Extra Bonuses for Book Buyers!

All book buyers of *Taming the E-mail Beast* will get access to hundreds of dollars worth of valuable extra bonuses, both from the book's author, Randy Dean, and from a number of highly regarded authors, experts, and speakers in related fields.

Randy is including access to a 60-minute audio podcast for book readers on Taming the E-mail Beast, as well as a PDF e-book he has written that compiles some of his very best time savings tips related to e-mail, software, office clutter, technology, and even at home.

He also has created a special "book readers only" web site that gives access to the hundreds of dollars of additional bonuses including e-books, podcasts, video files, and more, provided by a who's who of other experts and thought leaders. This "book readers only" web site also gives you access to several tutorial videos featured throughout the book to show you how to successfully integrate Randy's key e-mail tips into your e-mail activities.

To guarantee that you gain access to these valuable bonuses and the book readers web site, submit your valid name, e-mail address, and basic purchase information at: http://www.randalldean.com/taming-email-bonusreg.html

We will follow up your submission with information on how to access the bonuses, tutorials, and more. We will of course keep your name & e-mail address in full confidence and not share with others (as you would fully expect when getting a book on keeping your e-mail under control!)

D0150264

Testimonials

"If you want to be successful, this Book is a must! ... Randy has provided a powerful way to show you how to get more time back in your day to focus on activities that allow you to accomplish the goals that are important in your life. Great job, Randy!"

—Aaron Solly
Author of *"100% of What You Want in Life is Between Your Ears"*
www.BetweenYourEars.com

"An absolutely essential book you must read and apply...if you want to be even more successful in winning back your time and your inbox. The perfect book in the age of digital overload as I find e-mail to be both a blessing and sometimes a curse. I will be implementing several of the tips directly into my daily schedule!"

—Tony Rubleski
Author of *"Mind Capture: How To Stand Out In The Age of Advertising Overload"* and *"Mind Capture: How YOU Can Stand Out In The Age of Advertising Deficit Disorder"*
www.MindCaptureGroup.com

"Taming the E-Mail Beast is simply a must read for anyone who struggles with e-mail management and is serious about wanting to do something about it."

—George Beshara
Publisher, Managing My Life Publishing and Training Inc.
Developer of the Managing My Life series of Self-Study Programs
www.managingmylife.net

"Randy Dean offers ways to trim time spent online by using available tools and simple techniques that work. His book is

chock full of key ideas and practical exercises that will keep your emails from making you manic, providing systems for scanning, sorting, saving, and best of all, searching for stored missives if or when you need them. At last, here's some relief for those of us who feel awash in a wasteland of words!"

—C. Leslie Charles
Author of *"Why is Everyone So Cranky?"* and
"Bless Your Stress: It Means You're Still Alive"
President, TRAININGWORKS
http://www.BlessYourStress.com
http://www.WhyIsEveryoneSoCranky.com

"Randy Dean will indeed help you "Tame the E-mail Beast" ... and dramatically reclaim a majority of the time many of us waste with e-mails. Although he doesn't promote it, I also found many great marketing ideas in this book. You can learn all of these shortcuts yourself over the next few years or all at one time by getting this book, reading it and immediately applying this awesome collection of ideas, shortcuts and tips."

—Stan Billue
Certified Speaking Professional
Sales Guru and Popular Keynote Speaker
Author of the Upcoming New Book: *"Your Best Seller"*
www.StanBillue.com

"After writing my latest book, my e-mail account went crazy! ... I followed Randy's systematic process for regaining control of my e-mail, and now I'm back on top of things. Thanks Randy for immediately useful strategies for Taming that E-mail Beast."

—John Rowley
Bestselling Author of
"Climb YOUR Ladder of Success Without Running Out of Gas!"
www.johnmrowley.com

"Randall Dean's book has provided me with a new outlook on email and how I can assist my clients. ... Whether you know it or not, we all have a lot to learn about email. Randall Dean can teach you!"

—**Sara Bereika**
Author of *"Professional Organizer"* ADD Specialist and NAPO
Richmond Chapter President NEAT LLC
www.neat-organizing.com

"I had a feeling when I got [this book] that it was going to be excellent. What I did not know was that it would blow my doors off their hinges! The book was chock full of insightful strategies and tangible tactics to be applied immediately! ... I am a fully recovered "Blinger" and at ZERO EMAILS almost every day! ... Thank you for a phenomenal book! "

—**Jennifer Capella**
Introductions Expert and Certified Expert in the
"60-Minute Strategic Plan"
The Capella Group
www.thecapellagroup.com

"Randall Dean's Taming the Email Beast *is an unexpected pleasure and treasure trove of information...It is comprehensive, covering all aspects of email. It is immensely helpful. And it is full of unanticipated tips that can help the reader get on top of email management -- all in a format that dispenses information and contains a review at the end of each chapter. I would highly recommend this book to any professional who is dealing with ungainly email -- or dealing with email at all. Even if you consider yourself knowledgeable about email, you're likely to gain some pointers here."*

—**Diane Brandon**
Intuition Teacher and Author of
"Teaching Right-Brain Skills for Problem-Solving and Innovation"
Talk Radio Host: Living Your Power
on the Health & Wellness Channel of VoiceAmerica.com

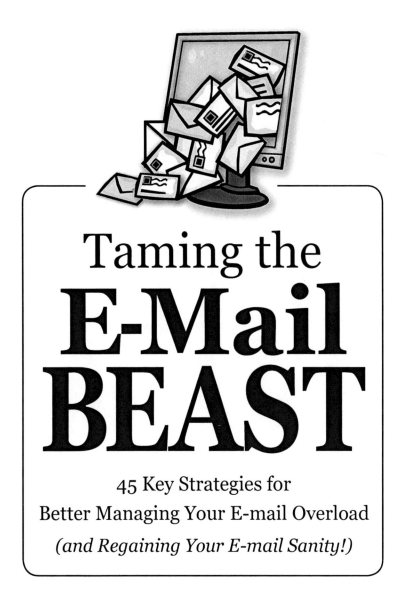

Taming the
E-Mail
BEAST

45 Key Strategies for
Better Managing Your E-mail Overload

(and Regaining Your E-mail Sanity!)

RANDALL F. DEAN

Sortis Publishing

Contents

Acknowledgments

There are many people that need to be thanked for their efforts, involvement, and activities related to the development of the Taming E-mail products and programs – too many to all be named (and if I've forgotten you here, please accept my apologies in advance). I would like to mention at least a few that deserve special mention.

First, thanks to all of my clients that have continued to encourage and support me in the development of the *Taming E-mail* strategies and systems. Your support over the last 4 years has made this "little program idea" into something of a powerhouse that just keeps going. A special thanks to my friends at University of Michigan HRD, Deborah and Kristen, and my friends at the University of Pittsburgh: Anne, Liz, Thomas, Rick, John, Kristen, Bill, and Cathy, for giving me some of my first opportunities to share this information. Also, thanks to Edita and Dawn at Michigan State for providing a big platform for the *Taming E-mail* and related Time Management/MS Outlook programs I've been able to lead for them – GO STATE!

I also need to give a special thanks to Geri for giving me the opportunity to start sharing these and other programs to association and meeting planner audiences here in the state of Michigan. Your continued support of my programs and presentations has opened up the national circuit for me, and for that I am forever grateful.

I would also like to thank Bob at the Michigan Chamber for opening up the Chamber circuit for me, and for his continuing support over the years. I also have to give a special thanks to Debbie and Carol with the ASTD for being welcoming and encouraging to that new and eager "content provider" nearly five years ago.

Thanks to Tony at MindCapture – you've been a great fan, supporter, and business associate. A big thanks also goes out to David Allen, *Mr. Getting Things Done*, for originally turning me on to time management and enhanced productivity nearly 20 years ago. You fundamentally changed the arc of my life for the better – thank you! Thanks also go to my former bosses, Linda and Jennifer, for both continuing to inspire me and encourage me as I kept alive my "little time management hobby" while working for them. And of course, thanks to Mike Webb at Sortis for seeing the potential of this effort and the promise of this material and tapping into it.

I have to also give a thanks to my current and former RDC&T team members: Carol Grainger, you've been a godsend and have helped this business jump to a whole new level – thanks for your calm demeanor, highly ethical behavior, and outstanding client service. You've truly enhanced this effort. Thanks also to my team of former and current interns: Kari, Megan, Kyle, Joe, and last but not least, Bridget. Bridget, I mentioned you last as you had to suffer through the first draft audio transcriptions of this book, and I don't know how it didn't drive you crazy! Thanks for your efforts in helping me get these ideas organized and on paper. Thanks also to Kate Petrella for her outstanding copy editing services – you make me look smarter and better than I am! Thanks also to Sharon H. and Todd Jungling for their efforts to give me a better web presence and make me a better web marketer – we are making great progress and I really look forward to seeing what's next.

I have to of course give thanks to my family. Mom, Dad, & Sis – you've always told me my dreams can be real if I go after them. Bill & Merillee – you've thrown out the stereotype of the "in laws", and have been huge in your support of us while I've been growing this business. Halle and Anna, you've made every day a wonder to be alive. I can't express how happy I am to have you both in my life. And Jana, without you, I can honestly say that none of this would have ever happened. You are my rock; you are my inspiration. I thank you all from the bottom of my heart.

Foreword

by Tony Rubleski

I'm excited for you today. You are about to retake control of your e-mail account, and eliminate one of your biggest personal and professional stressors. My friend Randy Dean has written the powerful new book you are holding in your hand right now: *Taming the E-mail Beast – 45 Key Strategies for Better Managing Your E-mail Overload.* In a world gone mad on information, this book is a must-have for everyone.

Knowing that Randy is obsessed with time management, and that he also originally became turned on to time management and enhanced productivity nearly 20 years ago by time management guru David Allen, the best-selling author of *Getting Things Done*, I was curious to see what he'd come up with related to e-mail. Let's face it, e-mail is both a blessing and can be a curse if you don't know how to handle a crowded inbox. The sense of overwhelm many people feel with e-mail shows no signs of slowing down, as the number of e-mails sent out per day keeps rising around the globe.

When I reviewed the advance copy of his timely creation, I immediately thought, "This book is not only valuable, but way overdue!" Here's a quick snapshot of what you are about to learn:

- Powerful ways to file and manage the onslaught of e-mail communication

- Clearing your active inbox to zero and the time savings you'll gain from it

- The "three-minute, one-touch" rule and how it can improve your productivity

- Why you should avoid "blinging" with your e-mail

- How to speed up your e-mail sorting and reply processes

- Better ways to use e-mail as a tool and not a distraction

- Why you should have three e-mail accounts to keep organized

Most people have hundreds of e-mails sitting in their active inbox, and this alone proves what Randy is saying and what the book teaches: effective e-mail management, while not a sexy topic, is a HUGE area of opportunity. Most people, including me, have never had any training or tips on how to use e-mail effectively. After I read this book, I made three immediate changes to my e-mail habits that have saved me a ton of time.

I'm a big believer in this book, and know that Randy also presents the book in a dynamic and simple way that makes you want to read it and act upon the suggestions he offers. Being an expert on "capturing the mind" of consumers, this book obviously captured my mind and has fundamentally changed my relationship with my work and my e-mail. I wish you luck and happy hunting as you chase down and tame your e-mail beast!

— *Tony Rubleski*
Author of the Amazon.com Bestseller:
*"Mind Capture: How You Can Stand Out
in the Age of Advertising Deficit Disorder"*
http://www.mindcapturegroup.com

Introduction

E-mail Insanity

S o, how many e-mails do you have? How many are just sitting in your inbox—read or unread—but are just sitting there in your inbox unfiled? 50? 100? 500? 1,500? 15,000?

And how many do you receive each day? 30? 50? 100? 200?

And how much time do you spend each day just reading and responding to e-mails? One hour? Two hours? Four hours? More?

If you are the average professional today, you spend two or more hours every day simply reading and responding to e-mails, and many people spend four or more hours per day on their e-mail. That is more than half of every workday!

For many of us, e-mail has gotten INSANE. It has become a "beast of monstrous proportions." It has taken away our ability to get our job done, as well as our ability to enjoy our job. How did it become this way? How did such a promising productivity tool become the most hated scourge of many professionals? What can we do about it? Are there strategies that can help us tame this "beast," and regain our sanity and productivity?

ABSOLUTELY!

With some sensible, proven strategies, some new habits, and some self-discipline, most professionals can regain control over their e-mail account(s). They can once again find the promise and utilize the power of this amazing productivity tool. And they can exert their influence on their co-workers, clients, and colleagues to help these people also regain some control over their e-mail beasts.

My name is Randy Dean. For the past 17+ years, I've been obsessed with time management and enhanced productivity. I've even become pretty well known all around the United States as the "Totally Obsessed" Time Management Guy, due to my humorous and highly useful training and speaking programs on time management, PDA usage, and related productivity topics. Over the last couple of years, I've also been getting known as the "E-mail Sanity Expert," due to a new program on e-mail that I've been leading—specifically, how to better manage and control your professional and personal e-mail accounts.

My focus on this topic area has been no accident. I've been leading popular programs on time management principles and strategies—for companies and associations small and large—for more than a decade. E-mail has always been a topic that we discussed in detail. It has been a standard part of my "flagship" full-day time management training program for busy managers, professionals, and leaders.

But over the last two to three years, I've seen firsthand how people's relationship and satisfaction with e-mail has changed dramatically toward the negative. My e-mail segment has become the most energetic, passionate, and even combative part of my full-day training program. Right when my course attendees should be falling into a carb-induced food coma following lunch, they instead get fired up and downright cranky when we dive into the intensive strategies that I share on e-mail management.

I've talked with my course attendees, and they keep telling me that there is too much e-mail coming too fast all of the time. They are tiring of the "immediate response" culture that has developed in many organizations in regard to e-mail. With the newer e-mail–enabled wireless PDA and smartphone devices, many are reporting a "24/7/365" e-mail reality—it *never* stops! And they are also telling me they do not have the proper systems in place for handling or managing the massive flow.

They are getting swamped—literally—by the sheer volume of messages they are receiving, and they are at a loss about what to do with all of it, or how to keep up with all of it. They are at wit's end, and are asking for (pleading for?) someone to help them find a path back to sanity. They want e-mail to be put back in its proper place—as an important yet not all-encompassing tool for enhanced communication and productivity. But they also desperately want this powerful tool to be used and administered in a much less reactive and "hyper-urgent" nature. They rightfully want to once again manage their work and their e-mail in a proactive and thoughtful manner.

It became very obvious to me that there was so much passion and need in this area that there was an opportunity to step up and develop a program that would help people once again regain their control (and their sanity) in regard to their e-mail accounts. (I found out that almost no one has had strategic e-mail management training—they've simply learned on an "ad hoc" basis over the years, thus allowing some truly sinister habits to appear.) They needed someone to develop tangible, easy-to-implement strategies—that can be put together into a comprehensive system—for sophisticated and yet very practical e-mail management, not just for individual performers, but also for working teams.

The *very* popular program on e-mail and information overload management that I've been leading throughout the country during the past couple of years has become what you are reading right now. Look at this book as your "map" to e-mail sanity. I've developed a regimen of 45 key e-mail sanity strategies and tips—strategies designed to "rein in" your e-mail beast. If you can follow most or all of these strategies, I'm quite certain that you can once again regain control of your account, and your career (not to mention your sanity!). Know now that the light is at the end of the tunnel—stay on this path and you will get there. We'll get your account back under control—one page at a time! Have fun taming that e-mail beast!

The Promise of E-mail

Do you remember when you first got your e-mail account? If you are like most professionals, you probably got that first account in the late '80s or early '90s. The Internet was brand new, and full of promise. Very few of us had any idea what it was going to turn into. So we started dipping our toes in the pool, and sending a few messages here and there—first to our co-workers, and then slowly out to our broader contact lists. We probably tested out an AOL account, and we just loved getting the "You've Got Mail!" message. It was so cool, and so new. Little did we know how this promising tool was going to develop.

Fast-forward to today. E-mail has become a ubiquitous business and personal tool for enhanced information sharing and communications. We now can correspond with individuals halfway around the world in a matter of seconds, and share not only basic text communications, but also video, voice, and multimedia-enhanced messages. Via attachments, we can send entire books, file packets, reports, photos, music files, video files, and more. We can provide active links to specific Web pages and Web sites all over the cyber-universe, thus allowing individuals to use your e-mail message as a jumping-off point for a cyber-journey to places unknown and unexpected. If we so desire, our e-mail can allow us to reach just about anyone in the world anywhere, and at any time. And with e-mail's close cousin, instant messaging (IM for short), we can even use a version of e-mail that basically allows for real-time communications across vast distances, without the cost of wired telephone services.

In a corporate setting, e-mail has undoubtedly increased productivity and enhanced profitability. It has allowed individual workers in different locations to coordinate work and share information at a speed not imagined thirty years ago. This has allowed for a very sophisticated globalization of business efforts in a very short period of time. Now, due to e-mail and the many other forms of Web-based communications, a software engineer in Palo Alto can coordinate with a software coder in Mumbai, a hardware plant manager in Malaysia, and a marketing team in New York, thus allowing work to move forward as if each of these people worked in the next office over, rather than on the other side of the planet. We can communicate more efficiently with co-workers, stay closer to our clients and customers, maintain distant relationships with family and friends, and do all of these things in a quick and relatively painless manner.

The promise and capabilities of e-mail make it one of the most powerful productivity-enhancing tools ever created. It is one of a few new information and Internet-enabled technologies that have fundamentally changed the way we do business and live our personal lives. And we won't ever go back to the way it used to be.

However, there is a dark side to this amazing technology.

E-mail's Dark Side

Most of us have never been formally trained on how to strategically and proactively administer and manage this tool. We've been expected to just sort of pick it up as we go. And that is just what we've done. We've picked up inefficient habits, lazy habits, and inconsiderate habits. We allow e-mail to run (ruin?) our day, rather than putting it into a proper place, perspective, and priority. We've allowed "urgent" messages from others to take us off of our required and desired paths. We've given our professional accounts to family and friends, and have burdened our accounts with tons of silly (sometimes funny) extra messages that cause us to work countless additional hours just to keep up. And many of us have seen our accounts get overwhelmed with spam and spoof e-mails, and are now spending too much time every day just hitting "delete" to get to the messages of real value and substance.

We've let our primary work account become an unmanageable beast. Many of us have hundreds (if not thousands) of unfiled messages just sitting in our inbox—some read, some unread—but all requiring some form of action (or deletion). Instead, we leave them sitting there—feeding, growing, stressing, and slowing—slowing our productivity, and reducing our ability to both enjoy and prosper in our work and our lives. We no longer know which messages are important and which ones aren't. And we can barely keep up with the new ones coming in every day, much less the old ones that have been there quite a while.

How do we regain control (and our sanity)? How do we tame our e-mail beast? How do we get back to the promise of this amazing productivity tool, and move away from the peril? These are the goals of this simple publication. Over the last few years, I've developed 45 key strategies for more effectively and efficiently managing your e-mail. I absolutely believe that if you incorporate most if not all of these strategies, you will find yourself significantly more in control of your e-mail account, and also more satisfied, productive, and fulfilled with your personal and professional lives. E-mail can (and should!) be a consistent productivity and life-enhancement technology; with some common sense and with a strategy, you can get it back to being just that. Let's start right now.

Some Quick Notes on the Structure of This Book

I don't want this to be a book that you just read and think about. Instead, I want this to be a book that you work with and interact with moving forward, thus allowing you to integrate the suggested strategies, new habits, and changes into your e-mail activities and your life. Because of this, I have structured this book with a few "value adds" that will hopefully allow you to better learn and retain the information shared.

1. End of Chapter Review Questions – Each chapter will end with a series of questions that will reiterate key concepts / ideas shared in that chapter. For example:
   a. How long have we been using e-mail?
   b. How much time does the average user spend per day reading and responding to e-mails?
   c. What makes e-mail such a powerful tool for potential productivity?
   d. Why has e-mail become an area of "pain" for many users and professionals?
2. Key Strategy Review – Each chapter will also end with a listing of the key e-mail sanity strategies shared in that chapter.
3. Video Tutorials – Book readers will also have access to a

series of video tutorials that are available on an affiliated book reader's web page. Simply visit this page, and you will be able to launch these tutorials to see how to actually use the discussed technique or strategy. (Some things are obviously easier to learn by actually seeing them vs. just reading about them – especially when related to utilizing specific programs and functions within software.)

PART I

**Daily E-mail Sanity Strategies
for the Professional User**

CHAPTER 1

You've Got to
Know Your E-mail Flow!

The averages are astounding—two hours per day, each and every day! According to John Carroll University and Forrester Research, that is how much time the average American professional spends administering his or her e-mail account, reading new e-mails, and responding to or forwarding e-mails. And a significant number of professionals report that they are often spending more than four hours per day just reading and responding to e-mails. That is more than half of a typical workday, just handling e-mail! This is why e-mail has become a beast for many of us. We spend so much time just doing our e-mail work that we can't get any of our "real" work done.

Now, when you go to the doctor because something is ailing you, the first thing they try to do is make sure they really know what is afflicting you. They do this by assessing your full range of symptoms, and then looking for the ailments that are likely to cause your symptoms. They'll go through a pretty rigorous process to feel confident in their diagnosis before they ever consider a treatment regimen.

I recommend that you too should do the same. Before you

can start to make smart, appropriate changes to how you are doing your e-mail work, you also need to first start by doing an effective "diagnosis" of your symptoms. You need to first study your e-mail beast before you can start to tame it. That makes sense, doesn't it?

By training, I'm an MBA. Many people often ask me what MBA stands for—here's one of my answers: Must Be Anal! Well, not to disappoint, I recommend a somewhat anal little process to help you study your e-mail beast, and diagnose your current e-mail situation. This process requires some tracking—and a little time investment—on your part so that you can really figure out what is going on. Sure, you could just skip to the next strategy if you would like to start adopting new strategies, but without doing this front-end assessment and analysis, you might end up missing what is really ailing you, and treating individual symptoms without actually "healing" your situation.

KEY STRATEGY #1
Track the number of E-mails you receive and the time you spend on them, to understand the size of your E-mail beast.

Here is the process that I recommend you follow. Try this for at least a few days, and ideally a week or more if you can:

A Recommended Process for Tracking Your E-mail Activities

1. Track the number of e-mails received on a daily basis:
    a. Track the number of professional e-mails received
    b. Track the number of personal e-mails received

   c. Track the number of e-commerce e-mails received

   d. Track the number of junk/spam e-mails received

   e. Track these numbers individually for any active e-mail accounts you have (professional, personal, and others)

2. Track the AMOUNT OF TIME spent on e-mail:

   a. Track how long you are reading and responding to e-mails

      i. Professional

      ii. Personal

      iii. E-commerce

      iv. Junk/spam

   b. Track how long you are filing e-mails/administering your account(s)

3. Tabulate the TOTAL TIME spent per day on:

   a. professional e-mails

   b. personal e-mails

   c. e-commerce e-mails

   d. junk/spam

I've created the following MS Excel tracking spreadsheet (next page) to help you with this process. (You can access this page on my Taming E-mail Reader Web site at *www. tamingemailreader.com*). I recommend that you go to this page, click the link to the actual Excel worksheet, and then print out the form or just save it to your computer and fill it out whenever you are working on your e-mail. This worksheet gives you seven days of e-mail tracking per spreadsheet. If you track for two weeks, simply use two pages. (By the way, one recommendation for you to consider when tracking your professional e-mails: also track how many of those e-mails are what you consider unnecessary CC's [carbon copies] or forwards. We'll discuss that in a later chapter, but for now, just get a feel for how many of these are clogging up your inbox.)

E-mail Tracking Spreadsheet

Copyright Randall Dean 2007 – All Rights Reserved.

As Described in Randy Dean's *Taming the E-mail Beast: 45 Key Strategies for Better Managing Your E-mail Overload*

http://www.emailsanityexpert.com

DATE	Professional E-mails		Personal E-mails		Unsolicited Junk/SPAM	Total Messages Received	Total Time Spent
	Quality E-mails	Unnecessary CC's/Forwards	Quality E-mails	"Jokes & Junk"			
Date:							
Number Messages Received							
Approximate Time Spent Processing							
Date:							
Number Messages Received							
Approximate Time Spent Processing							
Date:							
Number Messages Received							
Approximate Time Spent Processing							
Date:							
Number Messages Received							
Approximate Time Spent Processing							
Date:							
Number Messages Received							
Approximate Time Spent Processing							
Date:							
Number Messages Received							
Approximate Time Spent Processing							
Date:							
Number Messages Received							
Approximate Time Spent Processing							
TOTALS For Date Range:							
Total Messages Received							
Total Time Processing							

Observations/Ideas for Improved E-mail Processing/Management:

When you complete this process, you'll likely already have some ideas on how to reframe your e-mail situation. You might see that you are receiving too many junk/spam e-mails into your account, and need to talk to your IT group about better spam filter tools. You might see you are getting too many "joke" e-mails from your crazy Uncle Bob, and that you need to set up an "auto-file" mechanism for his messages. You might see that you are using too much time to write and respond to e-mails, and need to become more succinct. You might notice that Billy, the new hire in accounting, carbon copies everyone on everything, and that you need to go have a chat with him about that. If you see these and other solutions that are "no-brainers," GREAT! Enact them!

A Social Science Standard: The Hawthorne Effect

There is an interesting scientific research principle called the "Hawthorne Effect." Basically, this principle states that, very often, in human/sociological research studies, the sheer act of measuring a human activity with a desired research outcome may actually lead to the desired research outcome. What this means is that if you start to get very conscious of how you administer your e-mail account(s) and start tracking exactly how much time you spend doing e-mail, you might start to make positive, desired changes. You will consciously or subconsciously change your e-mail behaviors so that you are more efficient and effective with your e-mail.

You might become more ruthless with spam by taking the step of setting up filters. You might contact people in your personal contacts and have them start sending less "junk & jokes" to your professional account. You might start being more efficient in your responses, so they take less total time. You might develop better filing and archiving systems so that you can move e-mail out of your inbox to keep you from re-reading the same messages over and over. If you do these things, and many more, as part of your tracking/analysis process, GREAT! You are already receiving the benefit of reading this book, and ideally are already on your way back to reestablishing your e-mail sanity.

Now, if you have already started doing some of these things, I do not recommend you stop reading, as there are many, many more ideas throughout the rest of this book that may help you become even more efficient and effective with your e-mail. The key point is that you've already started to make some progress. Every bit of progress helps, so GO!

Analysis Questions Following Your E-mail Tracking Exercise

Now, let's assume you have finished your tracking process. The next thing you need to do is analyze the results. What are the outputs of your e-mail tracking exercise?

- **How many e-mails did you receive?** (Personal, professional, e-commerce, junk/spam, total?)

- **How much TIME did you spend administering these e-mails (reading, responding, forwarding, filing)?** Once again, break out by personal, professional, e-commerce, junk/spam, and total. (TIME is in all caps here because, in my opinion, the amount of time expended is more important than total number of messages received.)

Once you have this initial analysis completed, it is time to go in a little deeper. Ask yourself these questions:

- **Does this time usage make sense for my professional position and situation?** (In other words, does this amount of e-mail "fit" your position? Is it appropriate for your current position, or not?)

- **Does this time usage make sense for me personally?** Am I comfortable with the amount of personal time I'm

7

spending on my personal e-mails?

- **Am I spending too much of my personal time doing my professional e-mails** (ruining my work/life balance)?

- **Am I spending too much of my professional time doing my personal e-mails?** (More about that later—people can actually get reprimanded or fired for that.)

I always recommend that people do this analysis before doing *anything* else, because you need to know the answers to these questions to be able to effectively diagnose what e-mail ills ail you. Is it simply a matter of volume in your professional account? Maybe you need to find an outlet to delegate some of that e-mail. Or, is it something broader? Might you need to fundamentally change your behaviors and strategies regarding your e-mail to get it under control?

This is what the rest of this book is primarily dedicated to—changing habits so you can be more proactive and effective with your e-mail. Are you getting too many messages from your friends? Let them know you are getting swamped, and that you may not get back to them as quickly as they would normally expect. Also, ask them for their help, and request they stop sending so much junk. (Obviously, ask in a delicate, appropriate manner.) Are your family and friends bombarding your work account, causing you to lose productivity and efficiency? Create a new personal account, and have them direct their e-mails to that new account. In the next chapter we'll talk more about this strategy of having multiple accounts.

Regardless of what you see, start looking for and enacting ideas right away to change your relationship with your e-mail—professionally and personally. Look for those no-brainers and start to take appropriate action on them. As an author and creator of personal development books and programs, I would much prefer you read segments of this book and start immediately enacting the ideas rather than read the entire publication and only enact a few ideas. So, if you're inspired by something here, put the book down, enact the ideas that will help you, then come back and gather more ideas. If you've done that—if you've done some tracking and diagnosis of your e-mail situation, and have started to enact some smart no-brainer ideas, you are ready for Chapter 2.

End of Chapter Review Questions:

- Why is it important to track and analyze your personal and professional e-mail activities?

- What is the smart thing to do right now if you identify some "e-mail no brainers"?

- What is the Hawthorne Effect, and how can it have a positive impact on your e-mail habits and behaviors?

Key Strategy Review:

Key Strategy #1: Track the number of E-mails you receive and the time you spend on them, to understand the size of your E-mail beast.

CHAPTER 2

Have At Least Three!

No, we're not talking about beers or glasses of wine here (although that might make you feel better for a little while about your e-mail mess!) We're talking about e-mail accounts! This leads to:

KEY STRATEGY #2
Have at least three e-mail accounts.

Yes, I recommend that all e-mail users have at least three e-mail accounts. Three is a somewhat magic number when it comes to e-mail accounts for most users, as it allows you to separate work from personal, and it also may help you to manage and mitigate some of the flow of junk and spam e-mail.

Here are the three accounts that I recommend:

1. **Your Primary Professional Account** (this account you really stay on top of!)

2. **Your Personal E-mail Account** (this account you do on your own time)

3. **Your Internet/E-Commerce Account** (this account helps mitigate junk and spam)

Let's talk about all three.

1. Your Primary Professional Account

Here is where you do your business e-mail (and preferably only business e-mail.) This is the account that you give to everyone you do business with—your supervisor, co-workers, staff, clients, partners, business associates, vendors, professional colleagues, and so on. Give this account to these people, *and only these people*. Try to limit who gets this address, and keep it primarily designated for your professional contacts. *Do not* give it to family and friends (more about that later).

You want to limit your focus with this account to your work, and, if possible, only your work. By doing this, you allow yourself to maintain your focus on work activities and communications first and foremost. By limiting who sends messages to you at this account, you by design allow yourself to be both more efficient and effective when administering the account. You limit your focus to higher-value activities, tasks, and communications, thus allowing yourself to be more productive and more focused, which in turn allows you to create more value for your organization. Keeping your work account more under control allows you to have more work "sanity", and also possibly will get you home on time more often.

Why not give your work e-mail address to family and friends? The answer to this is simple. If you give this address to your family and friends, they will do something pretty crazy—they will actually send you e-mails at this address! I've done some tracking with messages from family and friends—they are almost never work related, and they are also almost never what I would classify as "critical content," meaning that they do not contain information that will help you do your job better.

What most people send via e-mail to family and friends

11

are things like birth announcements, wedding announcements, graduation notices, family gossip, pictures from the recent trip or vacation, and other "nice to know" information. They also often forward their favorite "joke of the day," or a funny/naughty picture (sometimes both), or even the funny audio or video clip they received from one of their friends. None of these things are directly related to your work, and many of them often will even distract you from your work—thus adding unnecessary hours per year to your time in the office.

There is an interesting reality to human nature—I've asked many people about this, and almost all agree—if you receive a message from family or friends in your work account, you are *very* likely to actually read it, even though you know it is probably not relevant or important to your work.

I've heard the excuses: "Sometimes you just need a humor break." "You can't be a work machine all the time." And, of course, "What if they really need to get in touch with me?"

My response to this is yes, certainly, you do occasionally need a break in your work. All evidence has shown that people who take periodic breaks in their work are actually more productive and focused than those who don't. But I also believe that many of us are swimming in information overload on a regular everyday basis. We are getting too many e-mails, voice mails, faxes, articles to read, reports to review, and so on. We're barely keeping up with the flood as it is. To extend the metaphor here, if the dam is busting, adding more water certainly isn't going to help stop the flood!

I believe there are plenty of opportunities for breaks, humor, and occasional distraction in our work as it is already designed. You'll likely get plenty of these from your office mates. (Have you ever seen the TV show *The Office*? How accurate is that for many of us?) Adding in an entire additional level by allowing your family and friends to regularly distract you when you're at work is often the straw that breaks the camel's back.

Let's take a look at that funny video clip sent by one of your buddies. First, as we mentioned above, you *are* likely to open it and view it. So, you open the e-mail, and have to download the video clip. This takes a couple minutes. Then the video plays, and that sometimes takes three to five minutes in and of itself (especially if you watch it two or three times!) Then, if it is funny, you feel obligated to send some sort of a witty reply to your friend, which usually takes you another two or three minutes. And then, if it is *really* funny, you have to also forward it to several of your other friends, taking another three to five minutes. Just add it up. That is ten to fifteen minutes of lost productivity, just dealing with this one funny e-mail. And if you're not on broadband, this all takes even longer! Four of those a day, and you may have lost an hour. So you are either an hour behind, or you have to stay an hour later to get the same amount of work done.

Remember this philosophy when it comes to personal e-mails: *I'd rather see these people in person than read their funny e-mails.* So try not to read these messages when you are working. (Better yet, don't even give your friends and family your work address, so you can't even receive the messages at work!)

But Randy, what if they really need to get in touch with me? First, e-mail should *never* be used as a primary communication method for critically urgent information or communications (we'll talk more about this later too!) You cannot guarantee that any e-mail message sent is actually received by the desired end user. You might mistype the address. You might have an Internet or server error either on your side or their side. Their corporate junk/spam filter might catch you. They might be out of the office at a meeting, training program, or vacation. And they might not have remembered to turn on their "out of office" reply, so you might not have a clue the message wasn't received. Not every message that doesn't make it through bounces back to your account—you may think it went through just fine and later find out that it never got there. Thus, e-mail is an *"open loop"* communications tool – the loop only gets "closed" when you know the intended recipient has actually read and responded to the message. Never forget this!

So how should they get in touch with you? How about the telephone? Or even in person? Yes, if family and friends may really need to get in touch, you should give them your cell number and have them contact you there. The most important people in your life should even get your office number. (But tell them to only use this when it is really important—regular stuff should go to your cell. That way, if you are busy, it will go to your personal voice mail.) When you use the telephone, you can be much more confident that a message was received. If they answer the phone, you *know* the message was received. Also, voice mail still tends to be a more certain connection than e-mail (although the communications loop is never really closed until your desired person responds or replies).

> *"Sometimes people are just*
> *paranoid. Other times, they really*
> *are out to get you!"*
> - Unknown

An Important Point: Big Brother *May* be Watching You

Here's an interesting fact—did you know that most courts in the United States believe that your e-mail account provided by your company is not your property, but is instead the property of your company? And did you know that most people have no inherent privacy rights to the electronic communications taking place in their work e-mail account? Court interpretations of the Electronic Communications Privacy Act (ECPA) of 1986 have basically come down on the side of employers, with most courts finding that e-mail monitoring of private sector employees by their employers is a reasonable activity within the course of doing normal business. This is due to the fact that e-mail is a two-way communication, meaning there truly is no "real privacy" in e-mail for a single person, and due to the fact that the employer is the provider of both the e-mail account/software as well as the electronic systems and Internet connections that allow for that e-mail to work. Also, many employees have used both e-mail and Internet to perform unethical and sometimes even illegal activities that often put their employers at significant litigation risk. Since the employer provides the e-mail service, with the inherent understanding that it will be used for the employer's benefit, most courts believe monitoring is reasonable, especially in the circumstance where the company has a specific policy on e-mail and electronic communications monitoring.

What does this mean?

Simply this—at any given time, any "higher-up" in your company may be tracking and viewing your electronic communications. (As a matter of fact, a recent study by the American Management Association found that nearly 75% of employers do some form of employee monitoring.) And, your employers can also quite easily watch what is happening outside of e-mail on your computer workstation (this should make all of you computer Solitaire players a bit paranoid!) Corporate spying on company employees is at an all-time high. Companies realize there are many valid reasons for keeping an eye on what their employees are doing while on the clock. Don't expect this to change anytime soon—a recent study showed that the average American worker wastes more than two hours per day at work on personal and silly stuff (Solitaire!) Companies are likely to increase their electronic monitoring activities, because monitoring may enhance profits and reduce litigation risk.

I'm sure a few of you are saying, "Yeah, but that stuff never happens. Nobody ever gets fired for what they are doing in their e-mail." Unfortunately, that's not true. Every day, people are dismissed from their jobs for using company resources—including their e-mail accounts—for personal purposes. In my frequent travels around the United States and abroad leading programs on e-mail management, I have now run into two professionals that have been dismissed due to inappropriate e-mail activities. These were the two that were willing to share their stories with me – I'm sure there were many more in those audiences that didn't admit to being reprimanded or released due to their e-mail escapades.

Why even bother with that risk? An easy way to avoid the risk is simply to not give your family and friends your work e-mail. Keep your work e-mail focused on work, both to maintain your productivity and focus and to avoid any problems with "Big Brother."

This leads to the second e-mail account that I recommend you have.

2. Your Personal E-mail Account

This is the account that you give to your family and friends. This is where you encourage them to e-mail you. Ideally, you will administer this account on your time, not on your company's time.

You can receive all the wedding, birth, and graduation announcements that you please here. You can view all the pictures and family videos you would like here. You can read every joke, and view every funny (even raunchy) video ever created, because this is your account, and you do have inherent privacy rights over this one. However, if you are logging in to this account while at your place of work during regular work hours on your work PC, you might be getting into a "fuzzy" zone—please keep that in mind.

And that is an important point to keep in mind. You should be reading and responding to e-mails received in this account *on your time*. That means before work, at lunch, or after work—not during work! You are not going to really help your work focus and productivity if you are constantly jumping between your professional account and your personal account during work hours. In fact, this might actually cause you more distraction and loss of productivity.

Because your personal e-mail account is typically filled with personal, noncritical communications, this account does not need to be managed nearly as tightly as your professional e-mail account. You still will want to follow many of the strategies that we will discuss later in this book regarding proper administration of your e-mail accounts, but your professional account is the one that I recommend you "Must Be Anal" with. Right now we're talking about your personal/family/fun/friends account—which should be treated as such. It is a resource that enhances your personal life, and should not be so time-consuming that it keeps you from enjoying your personal life. Have fun with it!

What providers should I consider for this account? I believe many of the popular Internet-based e-mail service providers are perfectly suited for personal e-mail accounts. Providers like Yahoo!, Google, Netscape, NetZero, Earthlink, and Hotmail (MSN) are great choices for a personal e-mail account. Often, these accounts are low-cost or free, provide lots of memory and storage, and are accessible from anywhere you have an Internet connection or can access a browser. I've been using my Yahoo! account for many years as my primary personal e-mail account, and I love it. It is a free service through my DSL provider, and they have given me 2 GB (gigabytes) of storage. That basically means I can save pretty much every e-mail that I receive and send for *several years* without running into space and memory problems. I can create multiple folders and categories for filing messages (more about that later), and take advantage of the additional services that are usually provided with these Internet-based accounts. One that I love is the "Bulk" folder, which automatically gathers incoming messages that are likely of a junk or spam nature, and gives you the option to easily select and delete these messages en masse.

Of course, these accounts are not nearly as secure as private or corporate e-mail accounts and servers—there are people who are pretty good at stealing user names and passwords—so I don't recommend you use them frequently for secure financial transactions and the like, but for the majority of the reasons that you would use a personal account, these work just fine.

These Internet-based e-mail accounts also make a great choice for the third type of account I recommend that most people have:

3. Your Internet/E-Commerce E-mail Account

The primary purpose for having your third account is to help you mitigate the amount of junk and spam e-mail coming into your first two accounts. This third account is the one you would use when doing the vast majority of your e-commerce activities. If you are signing up for a new Internet service, purchasing something new on eBay, joining a new online community, getting a new book on Amazon, or doing any other e-commerce-related activities, you want this e-mail address and account so that you do not need to use either of your addresses from your first two accounts.

That is because your e-commerce activities and the providers of these e-commerce services (and their related auxiliary providers) are a source of a good portion of the junk and spam messages that are generated on the Net. The less that you use your first two accounts for e-commerce activities, the more likely it is you will not be inundated in either of these two accounts by related junk and spam messages. That will help you keep those accounts cleaner and more efficient, since you will not be weeding through as many "junk" messages that are integrated with the real messages you do need to give your attention. And the more "hidden" and less public you can keep your first two accounts, the more likely they will not be captured by truly unscrupulous spammers and phishers (a "phisher" is a spammer who tries to capture your personal and financial data via the Web and e-mail to carry out nefarious activities, such as stealing your bank account information and passwords to do illegal withdrawals).

That is why you should do all you can to limit the distribution of your work/professional e-mail address to only those you are conducting professional communications with, and why you should limit distribution of your personal account to close family and friends. And you should ask all of them to do the same—be conscientious and careful with the use and distribution of your e-mail accounts (spammers and phishers sometimes gather e-mail addresses by stealing names off of other e-mailer's e-mail distribution lists, or by infecting someone's account with a worm or "Trojan horse" virus to gain access to their address book/contacts list).

Quick Tip: ***Tell your co-workers, clients, family, and friends to use the BCC field when they send out e-mails to groups of people.*** This is important because it adds one more layer of security to keep the spammers at bay—it makes it that much harder for them to find and use valid professional and personal e-mail addresses. When using the BCC, the recipients of the e-mail cannot see who else received that same e-mail, thus limiting the potential use of these e-mail addresses by unscrupulous characters.

"Ruthless" Administration. The beauty of having this third account is that it is an account that you can often administer ruthlessly. Think about it—no one that is truly important to you should be e-mailing you here—your professional and personal contacts should be e-mailing you in one of your other two accounts. The only thing you should be receiving in this third account is generic commercial correspondence.

Now, if you recently submitted an online order or joined a new Internet service or subscription, you may want or need to watch and read these messages. But if you know that you haven't done any e-commerce activities recently, you can be pretty certain that most of the e-mail you are receiving in this account is junk or spam. That means you can be ruthless in your account management and administration—possibly even mass-deleting large batches of e-mails without ever even opening them. If you aren't expecting anything important, and you know the people mailing you in this account are not direct personal or professional contacts, you can feel confident deleting these messages with little or no review. You can just "zap" them—delete them en masse.

If you don't have a third account, which means that these junk messages are getting integrated into the messages that you are receiving in your personal and professional accounts, you probably have to go through them one by one and open and review many of them. You aren't sure if they are junk or spam, so you have to check. You are likely to be much less efficient administering these messages, thus taking much more of your valuable time. Plus, you are likely to increase the risk of opening a message with an infected file (virus, worm, and so on). Having this third account helps take away some of the risk that would otherwise rest on your first two accounts. It also helps you find some extra time due to your ability to feel confident in mass-deleting junk and spam messages. (By the way, a recent study by SurePayroll found that less than one-third of the study respondents used three or more e-mail addresses – going "three wide" with your e-mail accounts is still a relatively uncommon, yet highly beneficial, strategy. [Source: NSA Speaker Magazine, September 2007])

Quick Tip: **Consider "Mailinator.com".** Have you found some information on the web that you would really like to get your hands on? Do you need to submit "a valid e-mail address" to get that information? Are you pretty certain the information owner will bomb you with junk and spam messages if you request the information? If so, check out this web site – http://www.mailinator.com. Mailinator. com offers instantaneous and FREE valid e-mail addresses for people wishing to make online submissions without using their real e-mail address. Simply use an "@mailinator.com" e-mail address, watch the Mailinator web site for the e-mail with your desired information, and get your desired information without the information provider ever getting your real personal and e-mail information. This is a GREAT tip for those looking to reduce junk and spam messages.

Should you ever consider having more than three e-mail accounts?

The short answer to this question: YES.

Some people should definitely consider having more than three accounts. There are two specific situations in which a fourth or fifth account might make some sense. Let's discuss each of these two situations:

1. You are a member/volunteer/leader of an extracurricular or external professional or personal membership group or association, and receive a significant amount of e-mail related to your responsibilities in this group or club. In this situation, you may not want the club e-mails to clutter up your professional account or distract you from your primary job focus when you are at work. But, at the same time, you may want to follow the same level of rigor with your club or group e-mail account that you do with your primary professional account. In this situation, having a second "professional" account for your group, association, or club makes perfect sense. You might check it once a day during your work hours, just to make sure nothing critical pops up, and then, when doing your after-hours work related to your club, administer this account just like you administer your primary professional account (the process of which we discuss in much greater detail throughout the rest of this book.) By keeping the messages related to this endeavor outside of your primary professional e-mail account, you allow yourself to remain focused and productive with your primary professional responsibilities while working.

2. You've got so much mail coming into your primary professional account that it is becoming problematic keeping up with the flow, and you have a designated

administrative or personal assistant that supports you in your position. In this situation, you could basically break your account into two professional accounts: account #1 is the general account that you give out to everyone in your professional "universe," while account #2 is your "super double top-secret" account—the account you only give out to a small handful of highest-priority supervisors, co-workers, clients, and key vendors.

Account #1 is administered on a regular day-to-day basis by your administrative assistant. He or she reads all incoming e-mails, responds to those that are simple in nature, and forwards to your second account those that are both important and urgent. He or she then prioritizes the rest of the e-mails received, and works with you on a plan for appropriate response (including no response or a delayed response if appropriate.)

When your assistant does respond for you, it should be clear in the outgoing messages that he or she is responding in your place (Dear Jill, this is Steven, Ms. Smith's assistant, responding to your message in her stead. Her schedule for a meeting next week . . .) Doing this alleviates the concern that may come up for some supervisors/executives that a word misspoken or a message misinterpreted will be taken improperly by the message recipient, or that an inappropriate message was sent by that same manager/executive.

At the same time, for an overwhelmed manager or executive, having this assistant shouldering some of the e-mail load helps to guarantee that the manager is being appropriately responsive to those contacting him or her, and yet is also meeting the productivity responsibilities of the position. This leads to a key final discussion point for this chapter:

Acknowledging "Overflow"

In Chapter 1, we discussed the importance of knowing your flow of e-mails—number received, kinds of messages received, and amount of time per day spent processing those messages. I spend a good part of this book discussing strategies that may help to mitigate a certain amount of e-mail "flow" issues—reducing the number of unnecessary CC's, forwards, and so on; strategies for reducing or eliminating junk or spam; and, as we've already discussed in this chapter, strategies for keeping personal and professional e-mails in separate accounts. I do recommend that anyone dealing with significant volume and flow issues with their e-mail account(s) adopt every strategy shared in this book that you believe will help your situation.

That being said, in my training and speaking programs all around the United States and internationally, I have run into certain managers, supervisors, and executives that have so much e-mail coming into their accounts that there is no group of strategies or total system that will "fix" their entire e-mail crisis situation. They have so much coming in so fast, requiring so much time and energy, it is simply a function of mathematics—there are not enough minutes in the day to keep up with all of it. These managers come to me looking for a "quick solution" to a fundamental job design problem. As I say to them, "Even if I can help you reduce your e-mail volume by 15 to 30 percent, it sounds like you are still getting hit by a fire hose!"

This is a situation in which e-mail isn't really the culprit—job design is. Your e-mail volume may be a symptom of a job over-designed (or under-designed!) You've got too much work for one person, and there are no workable solutions to this problem other than getting more help or eliminating some of the work. Usually, this isn't the answer that people want to hear, but it is often the truth—sometimes the hard truth. It is a hard truth because managers sometimes know that there is no help to be had—they do not have an assistant or support person to use as an outlet for some of their e-mail flow. They know their company's current fiscal situation will not allow them to hire someone to help, someone they can delegate to, someone to share the load of work with. Thus, they know they have a tough choice—keep working an 80-hour week, go find something else to do, or work less than 80 hours a week and not meet the basic performance requirements of the job.

This is a very difficult position to find oneself in. I've been there personally at least once in my career, and I've known several other professionals who also have been in this unfortunate place. Typically, people last in these poorly designed jobs for a couple years, before their mind and their body start breaking from the stress, and they ultimately make a move to something better. (And I do firmly believe that certain corporations have made this a "standard operating procedure." They give each individual a two-person job, because if you can get your employees to buy into this, you can certainly enhance short-term profits. The statistics on work hours by mid- to senior-level managers here in America, especially in larger corporations, bears this out. We're now working more hours with fewer people than we ever have, while many corporations are boasting record profits. This profit of course comes at a very high cost—not only to the overworked individual manager, but also to his or her family and community.)

But I've also known a few people who have believed they were in this situation when they actually weren't. They believed there were no additional resources to help them, but this wasn't true. If they had taken the time to diagnose the situation, diagnose the assets available to them, and build a smart and cogent case for additional resources (or just used the latent resources already available to them!), they would have found that their request for a change in the design of their job, the flow of their work, and the resources available to them would have been approved. (Perhaps they could have even made these changes on their own—they could have just stopped doing silly stuff they really didn't need to be doing!) And they would have found a much more receptive response from their managers regarding these changes than they anticipated. But they simply didn't ask. The next manager that followed them did, and got exactly what the previous manager was afraid to ask for.

Sometimes all you need to do when you ask is to show your supervisors your evidence that, after cutting out all the fat, you are still doing six hours a day of necessary e-mail, and that you also have six to eight hours a day of necessary task and project responsibility. They'll see you've done due diligence, and they'll get you the help you need. Unfortunately, you sometimes have to, as they say in poker parlance, "put all of your chips in". You have to threaten that you'll leave if they don't provide you the necessary resources to get things back under control so you can ultimately be successful. It is sad but true that there are some companies and some managers that will only really listen to you if you are willing to "go all in." But most of us are never really willing to go that far to effect the change, even though the change we desired could have been ours if we just asked intelligently.

If you are standing in front of a full-force fire hose, please remember that even if you adopt every strategy cited in the rest of this book, the force of the total flow hitting you may still hurt. The problem you are facing may be bigger than just e-mail, and if this is the case, you might need to go through the sometimes arduous task of documenting your situation and advocating for additional resources. But that is just part of being a competent professional—identifying when things are out of whack and getting them back in alignment. Or, you might need to acknowledge to yourself that you are in a no-win situation, and, for your own health and sanity, determine that you need to make a change.

Now, if you feel that you are not truly standing in front of an e-mail fire hose, and that you just need some help getting your current situation better organized, effective, and under control, it is time to move on to the next key strategy.

End of Chapter Review Questions:

•   What are the three recommended types of e-mail accounts most people should have?

•   What are the two key reasons you do you not want to give your family and friends your work e-mail address?

•   Why is the "internet/e-commerce" e-mail account important for maintaining productivity and focus?

•   When are two times to consider going beyond three e-mail accounts?

•   When is e-mail not the "problem", but the "symptom" of something much larger?

Key Strategy Review:

Key Strategy #2: Have at least three e-mail accounts.

CHAPTER 3

The Ultimate E-mail Clutter Buster

OK, so you've tracked the flow of e-mail coming into your accounts, and, if you didn't already have them, you've also created your new e-mail accounts so you can separate work/professional e-mails from your personal e-mails and e-commerce e-mails (and hopefully also the junk/spam messages that are trying to find you). Now, it is time to start diving into specific strategies that will help you better manage the flow and organization of your e-mail account.

KEY STRATEGY #3:
Follow the Three-Minute, One-Touch Rule

This strategy transcends e-mail and is one that I recommend you use for all of your information processing—all documents and communications received—in your work and life. It is called the "Three-Minute Rule," and is a strategy I learned nearly twenty years ago from David Allen, pre-eminent guru of time management and personal organization, and author of the books *Getting Things Done* and *Ready for Anything.* Basically, this rule states that you should develop a new power habit of looking at/reviewing every new piece of information that you have to process, regardless of what it is (e-mail, voice mail, snail mail, article to read, report to review, and on and on), and then you should quickly answer a critical question: Can I get the task related to this new piece of information completed in three minutes or less?

If the answer is yes, then your designated action—the new power habit that you want to develop for yourself—is to get that task done *right now*. Your goal is to learn to touch each new information input *one time*, and make this critical decision: If you can get it done now in three minutes or less, do it now! By defining and completing the quick little three-minute-or-less tasks that pop up in your life as they happen, you will by design greatly reduce the amount of "clutter" that can build up in your life (and your e-mail accounts!)

What you don't want to do is keep picking up and looking at quick little task reminders several times without getting them done. Most of us tend to let these little things pile up—we say, "Oh, that's quick and easy. I can do that later." But what happens is that, especially with quick little things, if we let them stack up, we end up looking at each little task several times before actually completing it, losing a minute or so of valuable time every time we look at it. After looking at it two or three times, we've just lost the time it would have taken to just get the thing done in the first place! Why let them stack up? Just finish them, and move on!

(At this point, some people will invariably ask me a question related to this: "But Randy, what if I don't have three minutes? What if I look at this new input, but I don't have three minutes to get it done right now?" My quick and short answer: if you don't have *three minutes* to get the related task done, you don't even have the time to look at it! KEEP YOUR FOCUS. Resist the temptation to look at these new inputs until you have effectively handled whatever it is that is making you so busy. Once this critical project or task is handled, THEN look at any new inputs that have come in during the meantime, and follow the specified three-minute, one-touch rule.)

Filing and Archiving Within the Three-Minute-Rule Philosophy

"Letting things stack up" is why so many professionals that I consult with have large piles of disorganized information and clutter in their offices and workstations. When analyzed, invariably, a significant portion of these items are three-minute-or-less tasks that had been "left for later". Had these people just completed them at the time they received them, most of the mess in their offices would disappear. This obviously includes things that need to be filed—filed in your e-mail inbox, your hard drive/share drive, and in your hard-copy files. Later in this book, we'll discuss e-mail filing strategies for how to better handle and file "completed" e-mails for later reference.

In *Getting Things Done*, David Allen shares strategies on how to build the proper infrastructure so you can file all forms of information, including hard-copy and electronic documents, so that you can become ruthlessly efficient and fast at filing. This process in and of itself can greatly enhance your ability to handle things in three minutes or less and also help you to keep your office/workstation clean and efficient, greatly increasing your productivity. If filing has become an issue for you, and is greatly affecting your performance, I strongly recommend that you read *Getting Things Done* right after you get done reading this book.

Here's how you know filing has become an issue: you spend a good amount of time nearly every workday simply looking for documents in and around your desk/office/workstation, and on your computer. You lose significant time daily doing this, and find it both frustrating and aggravating that you can't seem to find what you need when you need it. This would indicate a lack of appropriate "infrastructure" to handle your archival information. You *will* greatly increase your productivity and performance (not to mention your sanity and happiness) if you get this issue under control. For many people, simply getting their manual and electronic filing systems under control can save them an hour or more per day of lost productivity (that is not a typo – it truly can be an hour or more *per day*!)

The combination of the Three-Minute, One-Touch Rule with a well-designed, efficient, and coordinated filing system creates incredible possibilities for most professionals. They suddenly know how to handle the quick little stuff, and also how to clear out the clutter. They might actually get out in front of their work for a change, rather than being completely reactive all of the time. They also will exhibit a level of competency that enhances the confidence of their staff, since people will come into their office/workstation area and see a person that is "together." If you've ever had a boss who had an office that looked like a "paper bomb" went off, you probably had some questions about his or her leadership capabilities and professional competence simply due to disorganization. Invest the time and (not very much) money to get your filing and organization systems up to speed. You will be more productive and less stressed, and exude a stronger confidence and capability to get things done.

Three-Minute Rule as a Work "Flow" Facilitator

Looking at the Three-Minute Rule from a macro-perspective, if large teams and organizations had the majority of professionals within the team all following the Three-Minute Rule together, they would likely see significant increases in overall team and organizational productivity, simply due to enhanced workflow. Assuming that people are actually working on the right stuff, instituting the Three-Minute Rule would allow small things to move seamlessly and efficiently through the normal workflow process. The quick little reply you need from your manager to move forward on your project would come quickly. The needed e-mail with one small piece of critical information to complete a task would be sent. The fast and simple response that needs to be given to meet client needs would happen.

When managers and leaders do not follow the Three-Minute Rule, work-flow disruptions invariably occur. I equate this to a tree falling in the river (some would say a blockage in your arteries). If a tree falls in the river, the natural flow of the river is disrupted. Rather than flowing smoothly, the stream often begins to back up. Other things get "stuck" behind the tree, and much-needed resources from upstream don't make it downstream. The entire river suffers, all due to one dead log clogging things up. The same thing can be said for a manager who becomes the office equivalent of the dead log in the river. Ultimately, a dangerous flood may occur when the blockage finally clears and the river flows naturally again.

The dead-log managers let the quick little things stack up, and their entire work team gets behind, since things are not flowing downstream naturally. The team can't accomplish what needs to get done, because they are constantly waiting for needed inputs from upstream (the "clogged" manager). The entire organization can suffer due to this single workflow blockage, and multiple blockages (multiple managers or leaders blocking workflow) can often be disastrous to an organization's performance. It can also be just horrible for work team morale—people often sitting on their hands waiting for management movement, followed by periods of intense and stressful urgency when the needed information input is finally received, usually three days too late. Companies in this situation often face fierce competitive difficulties and high turnover, as individual high performers often leave for better situations, simply due to slow management response. Much of this could be alleviated if managers simply stopped letting stuff stack up and got stuff to people when they needed it!

Back to E-mail

So, the Three-Minute Rule obviously makes a lot of sense, and is something I recommend all managers, professionals, and leaders—regardless of rank or title—begin to adopt and follow as a standard operating procedure. (I even recommend you bring this little gem of a habit home if your home life is cluttered and chaotic.) Specifically related to e-mail, the benefit of following the Three-Minute Rule with your e-mail accounts is that this will help to keep your primary inbox for any of your accounts much leaner and more efficient. Ultimately, the only messages that will remain in your inbox at any given time are messages that still have a specified and unfinished action that takes longer than three minutes to complete. And if you follow some of the strategies that we'll discuss in the next chapter, you might even be able to move those messages out of your inbox once you determine what that action is, by listing that action in either your personal or professional task list for prioritized processing.

With your e-mail account cleaner, you'll be able to give appropriate attention to the new messages that you receive, and not risk letting something get lost in the clutter. You will be able to respond quickly when needed, and keep the work flowing through you. You won't have that constant worry that many professionals have: the worry that something out there is about to get you because you have hundreds or thousands of unfiled, unprioritized messages—many with active necessary tasks attached to them—sitting there waiting to jump up and bite you. You will quickly act upon most of those messages (or at least appropriately prioritize and task them), which will allow you to focus on the high-priority work that needs to be attacked and manage the work that needs to be relegated to a later time and lower priority. You'll also keep your team members much happier and more motivated, since you won't be the "stick in the mud" that causes them to lose their productivity.

Finally, you might actually give yourself the opportunity to feel reasonably caught up if you just clear out all of the latent three-minute-or-less e-mails currently residing in your inbox(es). Most of the professionals that I've worked with and consulted with have a significant number of three-minute e-mails currently clogging up their inbox, including those messages that need to be quickly filed. My typical first suggestion for most managers is for them to block some time on their calendar so they can have targeted time for processing and completing the identified tasks or actions related to the three-minute-or-less e-mails currently in their inbox. (How far would a half-day to a day of just doing three-minute e-mails until you are all caught up get you to feeling about your e-mail account? *Might this be a good time to put this book down and do this right now?*) Just doing this may bring back a significant amount of sanity and control with your account, and is part of the process we cover in ***Part II: Getting Your Inbox to Empty***. But first, we obviously need to talk more about what should be done with messages that take longer than three minutes.

End of Chapter Review Questions:

• What is the three-minute, one-touch rule?

- Why do professionals often end up under piles of clutter in their office and e-mail?

- How can following the three-minute, one-touch rule enhance personal and organizational speed and productivity?

- What is a "dead-log" manager?

- What is one strategy to consider doing right now? (Could you put the book down and get started?)

Key Strategy Review:

Key Strategy #3: Follow the Three-Minute, One-Touch Rule

CHAPTER 4

Make E-mail Prioritization a Priority

In the last chapter, we discussed the power that comes from handling the "quick little stuff"—including quick little e-mails—right now. There is no better way to reduce clutter and improve efficiency and productivity—inside or outside your e-mail—than to keep the quick little three-minute-or-less stuff moving.

But what do you do with those messages that will take longer than three minutes to complete? How do you handle those?

KEY STRATEGY #4
Prioritize e-mails that take more than three minutes

Once again, I'm going to refer to a strategy I learned from Dave Allen nearly twenty years ago. At that time, he taught a strategy that I believe still works perfectly today—simply take all of your more-than-three-minute tasks and put them in priority order, from highest importance/urgency to lowest importance/urgency. He even taught a system for doing this manually in a paper file system—actually taking hard copies of the information that leads to the task, and stacking them in priority order, with the lowest priority tasks/information on the bottom of the file, and the highest priority on the top. I still use this system today for all of my paper-copy information and related tasks/actions.

At the time, David suggested printing all of your e-mails that will take longer than three minutes to process—and then integrating those e-mails and related tasks with your other information inputs (voice mail, snail mail, faxes, articles to read, and so on) into priority order. Then, once you follow the Three-Minute Rule and also process all of your new longer-than-three-minute inputs first thing in the morning (and perhaps once or twice more during the day), you simply "work your pile" from top to bottom throughout the rest of the day, while also comparing it to your written task list. And if you don't get to the stuff at the bottom of you list, you really shouldn't stress—it was obviously the least important stuff to work on anyway, and maybe should have been put off in the first place!

I still actively use this strategy nearly every day. Why? Because it works! If you follow this simple process—clearing out your three-minute stuff, prioritizing what is left, and then attacking the highest-priority tasks, actions, and information, it is hard not to be successful. Think about it—you are keeping work moving while also working consistently on the most important and/or urgent stuff. Isn't this what every professional, manager, and leader should be doing on a regular basis? If you add in a forward-looking list of projects and personal tasks, giving you the ability to be not just reactive but also highly proactive, you can become seriously productive— and more important, effectively productive, meaning that you are working on the right stuff at the right time in the right way. That is productivity power!

Video Tutorial #1: *Printing E-mails and Filing in Your Priority File*

At this point, I'm going to introduce a special bonus for all readers of Taming the E-mail Beast. Knowing that some people learn better by seeing something rather than just reading about it, if you had any difficulty following the suggestion above, I have created a simple video tutorial that shows you exactly how I manage this process. I show you my actual working "Priority File", and how I take an e-mail with a longer-than-three-minute task and integrate it into my Priority File. This should help to make this process very clear and easy to follow. Visit the Taming E-mail Reader web site at http://www.tamingemailreader.com/videotutorials.html to see this and all of the other related video tutorials from *Taming the E-mail Beast.*

Really? Print all of your e-mails?

Granted, things have changed a bit since I took that class nearly twenty years ago. E-mail programs have become significantly more sophisticated. And we get a *lot* more e-mail than we did two decades ago, when e-mail was just becoming a popular business tool. If you get 100 or more e-mails daily (which is an amount that many professionals do receive), and if you print every single e-mail that will take longer than three minutes to complete, you might end up with a world-class stack of paper in and of itself! Plus, it takes time to print— sometimes quite a bit of time if your printer isn't that fast, or isn't located right next to you. But most e-mail programs have become far more than just e-mail programs these days—they have become what people now call PIM (Personal Information Management) programs.

PIMs not only allow for the receipt of e-mail, but they also allow you to integrate other popular functions such as your calendar, task or "to do" list, contacts/address book, notes, and memos—a "one-stop shop," so to speak, for all of your personal/professional information. Popular examples of these programs include Microsoft Outlook, Lotus Notes, and GroupWise. Even many of the Internet e-mail services such as Yahoo! and Hotmail now offer these services, and have become fully functional PIM programs.

A Paperless Option

Having all of these capabilities and functions in the same software program allows you to "toggle" between those different functions of your PIM program quickly and efficiently. Thus, you could use a paperless solution vs. "stacking" your e-mails, by using the Task function in coordination with your e-mail account. Here's how I do it (and this leads into a new Key Strategy):

KEY STRATEGY #5

Use "Drag & Drop" to create new tasks from your e-mails, then file related e-mails in your "Priority Processing" folder

If I get a "more-than-three-minute" e-mail that has a specified task(s) or action(s) that falls out of it, and I don't want to print that e-mail, I can instead move quickly over to my Task function and add that new task into my Task list. In MS Outlook and many other popular PIM programs, I can even "drag and drop" the related e-mail over to my task function icon, and this will cause a new task to be automatically created for me. Then, the original message text appears in the "notes" field at the bottom of the new task, and all I have to do is create an appropriate description for the task, and set the start and due dates for the task. In a matter of seconds, the new task is created and properly integrated into my larger task list with very little effort.

If I assign an appropriate priority and due date to the task, I should get to this task (and this e-mail) at the appropriate time according to my work flow and my other pending tasks, responsibilities, and priorities. The task will get done when it should get done (assuming that I don't have too much "flow" [too much volume] in my job—remember Chapters 1 and 2?) It will become integrated with my total work flow, prioritized accordingly, and acted upon appropriately. Very professional!

Once the specified task is added to my task list, you'll note that the original e-mail still resides in my inbox (no, it doesn't disappear from your inbox when you "drag & drop" it into your task list.) At this point, I want to move that e-mail out of my e-mail's inbox so I don't keep looking at it over and over (I've already decided what needs to be done), so I create a new folder in my e-mail account that I call "Priority Processing." In this new e-mail folder, I move any "more-than-three-minute" e-mails that have been added to my task list. A final tip: when you create the task in your task list, make sure to put the words "Priority Processing" (or just the letters PP if you are a fan of abbreviations) in the description field of the task, so you remember where the original e-mail that prompted the task is located.

Video Tutorial #2: *Creating a new "Priority Processing" folder in your e-mail's inbox, and integrating related e-mail tasks into your task list*

I have captured a video tutorial on how to create the Priority Processing folder in your inbox, and also how to integrate it with your task function. I have done this tutorial in MS Outlook, since it is the market leader in commercial e-mail programs, as well as in my practice Yahoo! account. (In the future, we may be posting tutorials from other popular e-mail software programs to add value for users of other PIM software.)

Video Tutorial #3: *Using "Drag & Drop" to create a task, calendar item, a new contact, and/or new note/memo in your PIM program*

I have also created a second video tutorial related to the above key strategy showing exactly how the "drag & drop" option works in MS Outlook. In this tutorial, I show how you can drag and drop an e-mail into your task list to create a new task quickly and easily. This same drag-and-drop functionality works with many of the other embedded features in your PIM program, including the calendar tool, address/contacts file, and notes/memo function. You can see how dragging and dropping received e-mails can speed up your ability to thus clear those e-mails out of your inbox – a great strategy for saving time and maintaining organization, discipline, and productivity!

Once again, visit the Taming E-mail Reader web site at http://www.tamingemailreader.com/videotutorials.html to see these and all of the other related video tutorials from Taming the E-mail Beast.

But I'm a "Paper Tasker"—Can I do this too?

What is a "paper tasker"? The answer is simple: that is a person who still creates paper-based "task" or "to do" lists. I teach programs all around the United States and abroad, and have found that there are still a whole bunch of paper taskers out there. You know what? If that works for you, don't feel a compelling need to quit just because some software junkie tells you that you should. Sure, the software can be pretty slick, but some people swear that within the framework of their job, it is easier to write a task list by hand every day, and then execute the tasks from that short and quick list every day. If it works for you, and you are doing well with that system, just keep at it.

If you still want to do the paperless e-mail prioritization option, you absolutely can. Create your Priority Processing folder in your e-mail account as already described, but instead of creating a new related task in your PIM-program task list, just write it on your handwritten list instead. Make sure to move your e-mail out of your inbox and into your Priority Processing folder, and don't forget to add "Priority Processing" or "PP" in the task description so you remember where the original e-mail now resides. Now, you're paperless too (except, of course, for your task list!).

By following these strategies, you should now have the ability to effectively prioritize the tasks coming out of your e-mails, either in hard-copy format, or via use of a PIM or paper task list. Just don't lose the key principle that resides within all of this discussion:

Prioritize those "more-than-three-minute" e-mails so they get done when and if they should. Then, work on the related e-mail tasks of highest priority, integrated with all of your other information inputs and specified tasks, getting the most important and/or urgent stuff done most of the time. (I'm hoping to make David Allen proud here!)

End of Chapter Review Questions:

- What is the proper thing to do with e-mails that have embedded tasks that will take longer than three minutes?

- What is the prescribed "old-fashioned" paper-based option?

- How can you do basically the same thing using a "paperless" option that utilizes the functionality of your PIM program?

- What is a "PIM" program? What are some popular examples of these programs? What kinds of functions do they typically provide?

- What is "drag & drop"? What are two examples of how drag & drop can save time when administering e-mails and related tasks/activities?

Key Strategy Review:

Key Strategy #4: Prioritize e-mails (and related tasks) that take more than three minutes

Key Strategy #5: Use "Drag & Drop" to create new tasks from your e-mails, then file related e-mails in your "Priority Processing" folder

Video Tutorials:

Video Tutorial #1: Printing E-mails and Filing in Your Priority File

Video Tutorial #2: Creating a new "Priority Processing" folder in your e-mail's inbox, and integrating related e-mail tasks into your task list

Video Tutorial #3: Using "Drag & Drop" to create a task, calendar item, a new contact, and/or new note/memo in your

CHAPTER 5

Create a New Habit: Check Your Accounts Only a Few Times Daily

In the last two chapters, we talked about strategies for using the Three-Minute Rule (that is, handling the e-mails that only take three minutes or less *right away*), and also about prioritizing the e-mails that take longer than three minutes so that you handle them at the appropriate time according to their importance or urgency. Now, let's discuss a management system/personal habit for your e-mail review and processing activities that allows you to give appropriate focus and effort to your e-mail account, be appropriately responsive to those sending you e-mail, and yet also give you specific periods of time for dedicated focus on the individual projects, tasks, and responsibilities that you need to get done. By following this system, your e-mail will be put in its proper place. Rather than e-mail overwhelming your work, it will become a normal part of your work. The basic strategy is quite simple, and is designed to get you out of the habit of checking your e-mail every time a new one is received (that devious and very damaging habit is discussed in Chapter 6!)

KEY STRATEGY #6
Get into the Habit of Only Checking Your E-mail Account at a Few Designated Times per Day

For most professionals, a good number of times to check your professional e-mail account is four times per day. If you are working a standard 8- to 9-hour workday, this means checking your e-mail every couple of hours. Obviously, four isn't a magic number—some professionals may need to check their account more or less often according to their circumstances, responsibilities, and situation—but it is a good general number for most professionals to consider.

Here are the four times that I recommend most professionals check their professional e-mail account(s):

1. First thing in the morning, as part of your "morning review" process.

2. About thirty to sixty minutes before lunch.

3. Right after lunch.

4. About thirty to sixty minutes before you leave.

Let's talk about each of these different designated times in a bit more detail, including the logic behind them:

1. *First thing in the morning, as part of your morning review process*, when you not only check and process your e-mail, but you also check and process the other inputs (voice mail, articles and documents to review, snail mail [U.S. Postal, UPS, DHL], faxes received, and so on) that have come in or have not been handled since the previous work day. Now think back: If you are following the system we discussed in the last two chapters, what

are you doing when you are checking your e-mail? You are handling the three-minute-or-less e-mails right now, and you are prioritizing any that will take longer than three minutes, either entering them into your task list or printing and sorting them into your priority file.

Obviously, for most professionals, just checking your e-mail one time per day, first thing in the morning, is not sufficient to keep up with the demands for your work and the needs of your co-workers, clients, vendors, and others you deal with. Most of us probably need to check and respond to e-mails more often than once a day to be "appropriately responsive"—to manage expectations appropriately and handle unexpected important or urgent tasks that come up. But also, we don't want to fall into that trap of constantly checking our e-mail, thus making it impossible to give dedicated time to individual projects, tasks, and responsibilities with a singular focus and our highest productivity and effectiveness. So, check your e-mail first thing in the morning, get the quick ones done and the others prioritized, and then spend the next couple of hours getting some focused work done!

2. *About thirty-to-sixty minutes before lunch.* It's been a couple hours since you last checked your e-mail. You've gotten some focused work done—moved forward some projects, had some conversations and phone calls, knocked out some tasks, maybe attended a meeting. And now, you have about thirty-to-sixty minutes before lunch.

Yes, go ahead and check your e-mail again! Now, don't wait until you only have five or ten minutes before you want to take lunch to check your e-mail—check it at least thirty minutes before. Why thirty or more minutes? Two very simple reasons: 1) If something really urgent or important has come in during the last two hours, you might need a little time to handle it! 2) If you've gotten several quick little "three-minute" e-mails to respond to, you need a little time to create and send those responses and/or handle those quick tasks (remember, we do not want you reading quick-response e-mails without actually making the response or completing the task!). And finally, you need a little time to appropriately task or prioritize any of the e-mails that need a longer response or include an embedded longer-than-three-minute task.

3. *Right after lunch.* You are just getting back to your desk, and haven't started anything new yet, so you aren't losing traction or attention checking your e-mail right now. Go ahead and check to see if anything urgent and important came in while you were out at lunch. Remember to get those three-minute e-mails done and gone, and prioritize/ task the rest!

4. *Thirty-to-sixty minutes before you plan to leave.* You've had a nice block of time to get some focused work done since your last e-mail check. But you probably should be checking to see if anything urgent or important has popped in since just after lunch. Once again, just as you did when checking before lunch, make sure you give yourself enough time to adequately respond to both the urgent/ critical messages and three-minute-or-less messages—at least thirty to sixty minutes before you plan to leave. (By the way, *never* check your e-mail five minutes before you plan to leave—that is when you often get "caught," and end up staying much later than you wanted or needed to because a last-minute urgent e-mail found you. I always recommend that you turn off your e-mail account about five to ten minutes before you plan to leave. And by the way, if someone sends you an e-mail at 4:59 P.M. on a Friday, is it reasonable for that person to expect a response

from you that day? I think we all know the answer to that question!)

Two Other Flexible Times You Can Check E-mail. In addition to the four "set" times just mentioned, there are two other, more flexible times during the workday when you can feel free to check your e-mail without a guilty conscience and without adversely affecting your productivity:

5. *At the completion of any significant piece of project work, before transitioning to something else.* If you've gotten a good amount of focused work done on a project or task, and you are about to transition to something else, go ahead and check your e-mail. Since you are between projects/ tasks, you won't be losing your train of thought or your momentum by checking e-mail. E-mail causes you to lose productivity and momentum when you let it disrupt your focus, but when you are transitioning between projects, this doesn't really happen—your focus has already been changed. If it makes you feel better, go ahead and check your e-mail. (That being said, if you are trying to have a truly productive day, you could just move into that next project and/or task and not check your e-mail—you might surprise yourself with how much you get done.)

6. *After a meeting.* If you've just finished attending a meeting, and you haven't started working on a follow-up project or task, that is also an opportunity to quickly check e-mail. Once again, your focus hasn't been directed yet, so it can't be interrupted, and thus you won't really lose any efficiencies checking your e-mail at this time.

Remember that for both of these more flexible times, the same rules still apply: three-minute e-mails should be dealt with immediately, and all others appropriately prioritized/

tasked. With these two flexible times plus the four standard times, most people will probably check their professional e-mail account five to seven times daily, or just about every hour. That should be more than enough to be "appropriately responsive"—and for some of you, five to seven times daily will be too often! You might want to stick to just the three to four set times so you can effectively manage your project and task responsibilities.

The Logic of this Strategy. The logic of this strategy is simple—you want to balance *appropriate responsiveness* with your desire for being *effectively productive*. You also *do not* want your e-mail to constantly be distracting you, thus causing you to lose your focus and your productivity. Being effectively productive does not mean being immediately responsive—it means getting the important and urgent tasks done in an appropriate and timely manner, and dealing with the less important and urgent tasks when they make sense (if at all!) My proposition is that getting back to people who send you "urgent" e-mails within a couple of hours is probably appropriate 99.9 percent of the time, and the strategy presented here will allow you to do just that.

What if you work in client/customer service? The strategy and designated e-mail times discussed in the previous section are for the "average" professional who is balancing appropriate responsiveness with normal project and task responsibilities. If a big part (or all) of your job is related to client and/or customer service, and part of that client/customer service management is done by e-mail, the strategy of four set times per day may not be sufficient for you. You may need to check more often—potentially every hour, every half hour, every quarter hour, and so on—to keep up with your job responsibilities. And if that is your job, that is fine! Check your e-mail as much as you need to in order to keep up with the defined responsibilities of your work. However, if your job entails significant project responsibilities as well as managing urgent client/customer relations, you must realize that you may be in a "no-win" situation in which you can never meet the needs of your position, your clients, and your projects.

If you are in this situation, you may need to have discussions with your management to find alignment. You may need to share with them the realities of your client/customer service responsibilities, including the amount of time each day taken by these responsibilities, and also the responsiveness expectations of these clients or customers (meaning how quickly they expect a response). Obviously, if several hours per day are dedicated to client/customer responsiveness, that reduces the amount of time that you can be expected to lead projects. This is of course common sense, but it is surprising how many managers tend to forget this simple fact.

The key thing here is alignment—if you are doing six hours per day of customer/client response, your boss needs to understand, and keep your project responsibilities to a minimal level. If your boss needs you to do more project work, additional resources need to be brought to bear to free up your time to do just that, and appropriately manage your client or customer needs—or, your work needs to be reshaped. Regardless, alignment is key, and often the first step is open communication with appropriate evidence to support your communication. (Remember the time-tracking exercise we mentioned in Chapter 1?)

A Little "Soapbox": The Culture of Urgency. Note that I put "urgent" in quotes when I explained the logic of the four-times-per-day e-mail strategy. I did this because it seems we are living in a somewhat unbalanced and unhealthy "culture of urgency" these days, especially in many corporate/ organizational settings, where it seems *everyone* expects *everything* right now. Of course, no one can be expected to get everything done "right now," but it certainly seems that some people in today's society and workplaces have the opinion that all of their stuff should be handled immediately. I fundamentally disagree.

The best managers and leaders know what is truly important and urgent, and what is not, and then they prioritize and take action accordingly, and their organization will support them in this working philosophy.

Any organization that does not agree with this statement is, in my opinion, very likely a sick organization that is probably in significant trouble. It most likely has a work and management culture that has lost control of the bigger vision and mission; is filled with managers who are not working toward the true end goal of building a viable, sustainable, profitable organization; and is dealing with unnecessary employee stress, burnout, and turnover. Patience and common human consideration seem to have been lost in many organizations, and my strong belief is that shareholders are not benefiting, nor are corporate profits improving, because of this. If managers and employees are not given the time to do an effective job, or the time to think about and execute the truly most important value-added tasks and projects that need to get done, how can the organization be as healthy and profitable as it should be?

If a culture of "immediate response, everything is urgent" prevails in an organization, it is fundamentally impossible for people to achieve the bigger mission and vision of the organization, as well as the related important projects and tasks that allow for that accomplishment. Some urgency is to be expected in any organization or business, but businesses that have an "always urgent all the time" philosophy are obviously either understaffed and under-resourced, or they have a poisoned culture. And, their top management obviously

51

hasn't taught the other levels of management how to pick and choose those activities, projects, and opportunities that can create the highest long-term value for the company, its shareholders, its customers, and its employees.

Urgency Bosses. Most often, it isn't the entire organization that views everything as urgent. It is just a manager or two who, for whatever reason, keeps tossing urgency bombs on the rest of the staff and co-workers. If you are that manager, you probably need to do some personal work to get caught up with your work and stop tormenting your team. (If not, you can enjoy having a revolving door in your department and a difficult time progressing to the next level, if not just keeping your current job.) If you work for that manager, it is never an easy situation; you may have to practice some active "managing the manager" tactics, to try to get your manager to stop dropping urgency bombs on your head. Obviously, this topic alone could create enough discussion for an entire book, so I won't dive deeply into this, but I will suggest a useful tactic:

A "Managing the Manager" E-mail Strategy. Related to e-mail, I do recommend one very specific "managing the manager" strategy: Let him or her know that you are following the suggestions in this book, and, in order to get your work done more effectively, you are only checking your e-mail at a few set times per day. Remind your manager that you are doing this so you can do your job better, which will thus make him or her look better. Ask for the manager's support in this—which means he or she has to practice consideration and patience when sending out e-mail requests to you. The manager needs to realize that you might not get back to him or her on the next "crisis du jour" for a couple of hours if that "crisis du jour" is sent by e-mail. And, if the manager absolutely needs to have something worked on or dealt with more quickly than that, he or she needs to use a medium other than e-mail (phone call, in-person visit?) to facilitate this. (Remember our discussion about the open-loop nature of e-mail in Chapter 2? We'll discuss this again in more depth in the next chapter.)

The manager *should* be doing this anyway – they should be confirming that critical/urgent tasks are being received by using a medium (or at least by confirming receipt by a medium) other than e-mail! To me, asking your manager to notify you of critical/urgent tasks by a medium other than e-mail seems to be a responsible and appropriate request from an employee to a manager. However, you'll have to judge, according to your manager (and including his or her personality and idiosyncrasies in the calculation), how to best request this change, and whether or not he or she will accept this request with good grace. Good luck!

This all leads into the next key strategy. . .

End of Chapter Review Questions:

- Why is it important to not constantly check your e-mail?

- What are the four recommended times per day for most professionals to check their e-mail?

- Why is it important to have programmed time for effective response to newly received e-mails (30-60 minutes before lunch and before leaving)?

- When are two other flexible times you can check your e-mail without negatively affecting productivity and performance?

- Why is it important to push back on organizations and systems that have adopted a "culture of urgency"?

- How do you adjust the recommended strategy if you are

an intensive client/customer service agent?

- What is an "urgency boss"? What is an effective recommended strategy for "managing this manager" related to "urgency bomb" e-mails?

Key Strategy Review:

Key Strategy #6: Get into the Habit of Only Checking Your E-mail Account at a Few Designated Times per Day

CHAPTER 6

Don't Bling!

This is going to be one of the shortest chapters in the book, but it is perhaps the most critical chapter when it comes to effectively managing e-mail and allowing yourself to be an effective, productive professional. The title of the chapter says it all—"Don't Bling."

KEY STRATEGY #7
Don't Bling!

Now you are probably wondering, "What does 'bling' have to do with e-mail?" In this forum, it has no relation to the shiny body adornments worn by the hip-hop faithful.

I'm actually trying to add a new definition of this word to the English language. Here it is: Blinger—person who immediately jumps to the computer and drops everything he or she was looking at, working on, or giving focus to, upon hearing the little "bling" sound that the e-mail program makes to announce that there is a new e-mail message.

Are you a blinger? Do you immediately drop everything the minute you hear that little noise? Or if you're an AOL user, the minute you hear "You've got mail?" If you are dropping what you're doing and losing your focus and direction because you are constantly jumping over to check for new e-mail messages, you are, by your own design, filling your life and your consciousness with distractions and interruptions. You are also making it nearly impossible to get any kind of high-value work completed in a timely and focused manner.

Blinging is one of the worst professional habits you can possibly have when you're trying to be a productive, project-oriented professional. It is productivity poison—and that's not just according to me. Listen to the experts. Recently, the University of London's Institute of Psychiatry completed a study that showed that people who "blinged," meaning people who constantly checked their voice mail, snail mail, text messages—and of course e-mail—suffered a tangible short-term hit to their IQ of 10 points. Read that again: their IQ was effectively 10 points lower when they were going through intensive multi-tasking behavior (such as blinging) than when they were able to have a more normal level of focus.

To put that in perspective, the researchers noted that a 10-point drop in your IQ is roughly equivalent to missing an entire night's sleep, and is more than double the 4-point loss that you get from smoking marijuana. (Reference for this information: *Yoga Journal*.) This is a fascinating statistic to me. Basically, if you are constantly checking your e-mail when messages come in, as well as taking phone calls, walk-ins, faxes, IM—whatever it is you're doing—you're making yourself more than twice as dumb as you would be if you just stopped and started smoking pot!

Please pause for a moment and reflect on this fact.

And here's an even more interesting fact: the researchers followed up and found that the effects of this "blinging behavior" are even worse for men than for women, because men have more difficulty multi-tasking than women do. So men are probably taking an even bigger temporary IQ hit than just 10 points. That means men especially need to be conscious of and cautious of this multi-tasking/blinging behavior. Here's the good news—it is a *temporary* IQ loss. If you stop blinging, you can pretty much immediately regain your lost smarts!

(By the way, a recent study by SurePayroll found that a good number of us have "gotten the memo" on the negative effects of "blinging". Fully 30% of small business owners only check their e-mail 1-4 times per day – that is very good behavior. But another 25% admit to checking their e-mail *more than 20 times per day!* This is that damaging blinging behavior that draws down your IQ, increases your stress, and kills your productivity. Break the cycle! [Source: NSA Speaker Magazine, September 2007])

Just as we discussed in the last chapter, there is absolutely no good reason to be a blinger unless you have people in your direct management/supervisory chain who have (unreasonable!) expectations for you to be constantly checking for their e-mails. That's the only *temporarily* valid reason to bling, but it is still a very damaging habit for long-term productivity and e-mail sanity. Blinging as a behavior is only appropriate until you are able to inform your supervisor about how damaging it is for your personal productivity. Once informed, your boss should encourage you to never bling again—and, yes, you should communicate with your supervisor to try to end this negative habit. Ask your boss to inform you by phone or in person if he or she sends you an urgent e-mail, so you don't have to scan every message coming in to see if it is from that person. Remind your supervisor that hundreds of other people send you e-mails, and that if you have to look at every message you receive from all of these senders just to see if it is an urgent message from him or her, you are likely spending all day constantly checking your e-mail and getting more stupid by the minute for it!

E-mail Is *Not* a Closed-Loop Communications Device.

Here's another key reason to make this request: What if you aren't there? What if you cannot receive the message? What if you are out sick, or on vacation, or caught in traffic? What if your company's server malfunctions and the e-mail gets delayed, or, worse yet, never gets through? This stuff happens—*every day.* E-mail is not a closed-loop communications tool. When people assume it is, they can get burned! When they assume that every message they send seamlessly and immediately goes through and is automatically received and opened, they are assuming a lot! If the message truly is urgent, and it is not properly received, the sender is the one ultimately on the hook for not following through and confirming receipt. Just sending a message does not relieve your ownership and responsibility—you have to make sure it got there, make sure it was understood properly, and make sure the receiver took the appropriate designated action.

If those things don't happen, the sender *should* be the person to take the fall. (I know it doesn't work this way many times, but it should work this way!) If you send an urgent message via e-mail, you have a professional responsibility to close the communication loop.

So, if you think about it, asking this of your supervisor (or of anyone else you know that partakes in unreasonable e-mail behavior) is appropriate in just about any situation, and is something that all good managers/leaders should understand and honor. They want you to be at your best, most productive, and most intelligent. That allows you to do better work for them, which thus allows him or her to perform better also. Why would they ever continue a behavior that they know lessens the effectiveness and satisfaction of their employees (other than just being mean-spirited)? If they don't get it, let them borrow this book, and encourage them to read this chapter. Better yet, have them buy this book too!

Here's what I suggest: If you are working on your e-mail, work only on your e-mail and keep your focus on your e-mail. You can look at new messages, follow the Three-Minute Rule/priority processing system we discussed earlier, and be critically efficient and effective at your e-mail administration.

If you hear that "bling" noise when you are in the middle of a project or activity, and it is not one of your designated times during the day to check your messages, resist the temptation! Stay on target, stay on task, and keep your focus on the project that you're working on. And if that is almost impossible for you, and you just can't help yourself, then: a) turn off that blinging sound; b) completely turn off the sound on your computer so you don't hear any distracting noises; or c) don't even have your e-mail tool open—keep it closed! Only open it up at the designated and specified times to check your messages.

If you can follow this one simple strategy, you're going to suddenly find that your ability to focus and take deep action on important projects and tasks magnifies immensely. (I'm a big believer of the productivity value brought from *single-tasking*!) You will also find your satisfaction increasing and your stress on the job going down dramatically, because you can maintain your focus, which always helps with getting things done. More done, less stress—that's a pretty good deal. So don't bling!

If you have people in your office who are blingers—especially people who work for you—teach them to stop blinging also. Make it a requirement that they stop blinging. Make it something they can be reprimanded for if they are caught. You need to help them break this habit because their lack of performance and productivity will reflect poorly upon you as their manager. Your team will perform worse if they are consistently engaging in this behavior.

Of course, as mentioned in previous chapters, if the employees are customer service and client service representatives, their job potentially *is* to bling. But even if that is the case, these customer/client service professionals should still be taught to handle each e-mail one at a time, and also follow rigorously the three-minute and prioritization rules, rather than blinging between e-mails and losing significant productivity due to a lack of appropriate focus on the individual tasks at hand. If they follow this process, they will likely handle each individual e-mail more efficiently and effectively, and will be able to not only handle more e-mails throughout the day, but also will handle those e-mails more professionally. In essence, by following this recommended process, they are "micro-single-tasking"—treating each individual e-mail as a single task with singular focus and attention.

Blinging Bosses. If your supervisor is a chronic blinger, share with him or her—in a humorous way if you can—what I shared with you about how blinging makes you stupid (remember: "dumber than a pot smoker"). Let him or her know that you are reading this book, and that it opened your eyes because you realized that it was negatively affecting both your intelligence and your performance. Ideally, that will make your supervisor realize that this bad habit is also making him or her dumb. And it will obviously add fuel to your argument of why it is so critical that your supervisor not expect you to be immediately responsive with e-mail.

If you are the boss, and can get yourself into this "no blinging" habit, as well as get the people around you to adopt this habit, you will see not only a massive productivity improvement, but also a massive job satisfaction improvement for most of your employees, as they will no longer feel as rushed or harried and they may actually be able to focus and *get things done.* You may see both less stress and less turnover in your team, department, and/or organization. Of course, higher productivity, lower stress, and lower turnover positively affects the bottom-line profitability of your organization. It certainly seems to be a no-brainer. Make "no blinging" rule number one in your organization and your work team.

End of Chapter Review Questions:

- What is "blinging"?

- Why is blinging such a negative habit for sustained productivity and focus?

- How many IQ points do you lose when you are actively blinging?

- Why is e-mail considered an "open loop" form of communication? And why is it important to follow through on urgent and important e-mails that you send to others?

- What is the recommended advice to follow when dealing with a "blinging" boss?

Key Strategy Review:

Key Strategy #7: Don't Bling! (Don't constantly check your e-mail throughout the day.)

CHAPTER 7

Build a Smart and Efficient E-mail Filing System

In the last few chapters, we talked about several strategies that are going to help you greatly impact your e-mail sanity for the better. We talked about following the three-minute rule and handling the quick little e-mails right now; we talked about avoiding the temptation to "bling" and read e-mails immediately; we discussed figuring out where your e-mail is coming from and dividing that up among your professional, personal, and Internet/E-commerce accounts. With these strategies, you should be able to handle most of your incoming e-mail more appropriately and efficiently.

Let's assume that you've got these strategies in place and you are getting down to focusing on your professional e-mails. You are probably at a point now where you are asking yourself a critical question: "What do I do with an e-mail that is one I want to keep, but is also one where I've already 'done what needs to be done' with it?" (In other words, you've completed the task, you've made the necessary response/ reply, you've forwarded it to the appropriate person, and there is really nothing left to do with that e-mail, except to keep it for future reference and archival purposes.) Well, obviously the appropriate thing to do is build yourself an appropriate e-mail filing structure and system. Why do you want to do this? Think two simple words: *clarity* and *cleanliness*. Once you get "done" with an e-mail, you want to make one of two simple choices: 1) if you don't need it, delete it, or 2) if you want to keep it for future reference, file it. Always following one of these two simple choices should enable you to quickly and efficiently move "completed" e-mails out of your inbox, thus keeping the inbox clean and allowing you to be fully clear on what truly needs to be worked on.

Why file? In short, you don't want to keep completed e-mails just sitting in your e-mail inbox, because if they stay in your inbox, there is a very strong likelihood that you will read these messages over and over and over again even though you've already done what needs to be done with them. Every time you reread a "done" message, you are wasting time. If you do that several times per day (which adds up to thousands of times per year!), you are losing countless hours in a completely wasteful and unproductive activity. If you can move these completed e-mails out of your inbox (and thus out of your line of sight), you will know that the only things that are still in your inbox are things that are still "open," meaning that they need to be dealt with in some manner or form. You won't spend your time rereading completed work (which, when you think about it, is a pretty crazy way to spend your workday!)

So, you need a system—a structure—to get them moved out of your inbox and into another place, so that you can reference them later if needed. Related to this, you also want to be able to move these e-mails quickly, efficiently, and seamlessly out of your inbox, so you aren't spending all of this newfound time filing your e-mails instead of rereading them, thus trading one time loss for another! You also want to give yourself the ability to quickly and easily find those e-mails in the future if for any reason you want to review them for needed information.

What this requires is that you build an "e-mail filing infrastructure." (Here's where you can tell I'm an MBA by training—"infrastructure" is just a fancy word for the electronic filing system you will create in your e-mail software tool that will allow you to effectively and efficiently file your messages.) For my primary professional e-mail account, I'm a Microsoft Outlook user, and it is quite easy to build this infrastructure in MS Outlook, but most of the other commercial e-mail programs—including Lotus Notes and GroupWise—allow you to do this too. Even the Internet tools like Yahoo! Mail and Google's Gmail will allow you to do this to some extent. They allow you to build folders—folders within your e-mail account—that allow you to move messages so that they do not distract your attention when you are working in your inbox.

And it is through the use of these electronic file folders that can greatly increase your e-mail sanity and your e-mail productivity. By moving old "completed" messages out of your inbox, you can keep your focus on your new messages and messages that still require action. The philosophy is that the only thing you want in your inbox is active e-mail—e-mail that still needs a task to be completed, no matter how simple or large. (And yes, I know that there may be times when you read a message and identify the task involved, but can't complete the task right away. Remember that in Chapter 5, you learned a strategy for moving these e-mails out of your inbox and into your designated "Priority Processing" folder.) We're going to build on that strategy/philosophy for e-mail organization and management here.

KEY STRATEGY #8

Create a personalized e-mail file folder infrastructure

To create my e-mail infrastructure, I've actually utilized some of the basic tools in Microsoft Outlook that allow me to easily create new electronic folders. In Outlook, creating folders is quite easy, as it is in most other commercial e-mail programs. Here's how you do this in Outlook on a PC:

- Mouse over the top-level folder that you want to create a new folder inside of (in this case it would be the actual inbox)

- Then, right-click on this folder and you will be given several options, including the option to create a new folder within your inbox.

- Left-click on the "New Folder" option, type in the desired name of this new folder (typically the project or person related to the e-mail you plan on filing), and hit "OK." You've just created a new folder!

Video Tutorial #4: *Creating a new electronic file folder in MS Outlook and Yahoo!(and moving messages from your inbox into an e-mail file folder).*

Obviously, this tip is well suited for a video tutorial, so please go to my Taming E-mail Reader web site at http://www.tamingemailreader.com/videotutorials.html. Here, you'll see how to create new folders in both MS Outlook and also in Yahoo! e-mail. (We'll even show you how to then move a message from your Outlook inbox into a subfolder.) And a very similar folder creation technique should allow you to create folders in most if not all of the other commercial and Internet-based e-mail programs/services.

By using the "New Folder" option, you can create as many folders as you would like inside of your inbox. It is in these folders that you put the messages you want to keep, but that you also don't want to keep rereading over and over again!

Here is a re-creation of the folders I am using in my current MS Outlook account (specific client names have been hidden for obvious reasons):

Here is my top-level folder hierarchy:

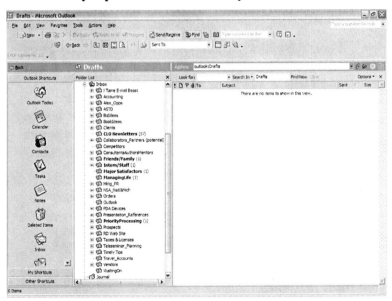

Microsoft product screen shot(s) reprinted with permission from Microsoft Corporation.

One nice thing about the Outlook file structure system is that you can even create folders inside of folders. You can actually build a pretty sophisticated file structure system for your e-mail. Related to that, here's what I have done:

I use my first-level folders—the folders that I created directly in the "Inbox" folder (what you see to the left) — to be my general topic folders. Some of the categories that I have in this top level of folders are things like "Clients," "Prospects," "Vendors," "Marketing/PR," "Contacts," "Key Colleagues," "Competitors," "Professional Associations," "Projects," and so on; all are things that make sense from a top-level perspective. As I first start building and using my e-mail filing infrastructure, I will probably file most of my messages directly in these top-level folders. But once these folders start getting a bit cluttered, or if it seems that I need more organization/structure, I will start to create folders inside of folders.

• In these second-level folders, I get even more specific. I name the specific projects I am working on, the individual clients or vendors I work with, the individual associations that I belong to, the individual competitors I am tracking, and so on, and create a folder for each one of those people/ projects/companies, so that I can file the messages specific to them directly into those named electronic folders. Note: When I create second-level folders, I typically quickly review and move all previous messages sitting in my top-level folders into the appropriate second-level folders, so I do not have e-mails related to the same projects/people/ companies located in two different places.

• Then I can go one or even two levels deeper if I like. A third level could be related to specific projects for an active client or vendor, or subprojects within a larger project. Let's say that I do work for several different departments/ groups/units for a single client (I do this for several of my clients). Under the second-level folder named for that client (within the first level "Clients" folder), I would have a series of folders for each of the individual groups, departments, or divisions within that client organization. That allows me to file the e-mails for each of these different operating units in a smart, appropriate manner. Then I can quickly reference related e-mails specific to any of those operating units in a sensible and efficient manner. If I know that I have an e-mail that comes from a specific department within a specific client, then I can quickly go into my folder structure and find that e-mail and its related information.

This is an excellent time to stop reading, go into your e-mail software tool, and start creating appropriate folders and subfolders.

You can see my list of top-level folders in the accompanying screen capture from my working version of MS Outlook. Of course, these top-level folders are appropriate for me and my business, and you'll need to create folders that are more specific to you and your professional situation. Use my list as an idea starter. It might even make sense for you to take out a scratch piece of paper, and jot down your ideas for the folders that will be most useful for you. Then, once you are comfortable with the new folders you would like to create, stop reading, and create them! One final note on this: Don't worry about building the "perfect" e-mail infrastructure on your first try—the software you are using is flexible enough to allow for changes downstream. Just give it your best effort, build your folders, and get ready to start filing messages!

Example of "folders inside of folders"

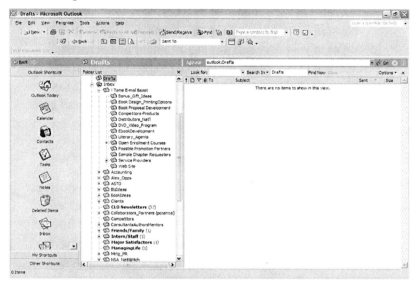

Microsoft product screen shot(s) reprinted with permission from Microsoft Corporation.

Moving Messages and Folders: Mouse, Hold, Drag, and Drop

If you've created your folder structure, and are ready to start moving messages, remember that moving a message in MS Outlook (and most other commercial e-mail systems) is as easy as "drag and drop." This capability was featured back in Chapter 4 in the "drag and drop" video tutorial (#3), as well as in this chapter's video tutorial on folder creation. To drag and drop a message from you inbox into another subfolder, simply mouse over the message you would like to move, hold down the left-click button on your mouse, and then drag and drop the message into the desired new folder. You can move messages from your inbox to any of your subfolders, and also move messages back and forth between the individual subfolders. (By the way, you can use the exact same "mouse, hold, drag, and drop" strategy to move not just messages, but you can also move e-mail folders too!)

Now, if you are getting antsy to start cleaning up all of the messages in your account, it is important for you to remember that the next two chapters outline the process I recommend for cleaning up your account and your existing unfiled messages. That being said, if you can't help yourself, go right ahead and start creating folders and filing messages!

Moving Misfiled Messages and Folders

As you can see from the previous paragraphs, creating folders and moving messages and folders is quite easy. Accidentally misfiling messages into the wrong folders is equally easy. Every once in a while, I'll get moving too fast, or my computer might be running a tad slow, and I'll accidentally drop a message or folder in the wrong place. If I do, no big deal! Simply open up the folder that the misfiled message or folder was inadvertently dropped into, and use the "mouse, hold, drag, and drop" technique to move the e-mail or folder back into its proper place.

These techniques should similarly work for the other PC-based commercial e-mail tools. A similar set of techniques should also work for Mac-based systems, although the left- and right-clicking obviously will not work on a Mac system.

Web-Based E-mail Systems

Most of the online, Web-based e-mail systems such as Yahoo! Mail, Gmail, and Hotmail do allow you to also build subfolders within your account, but they often don't allow you to build the same depth of structure. Usually, you are only allowed to have top-level folders, and you can't really create folders within folders. When using a Web-based e-mail system, you might have to be a little more concise with the number of folders that you are creating, so you can keep the organizational structure reasonable and sensible. I typically use these Web-based online systems for my personal account and also my Internet account (for e-commerce activities), and thus don't want or need as robust a structure as I do for my professional account. I have many fewer folders in either of these accounts than in my professional account, and that is just fine. (I'm actually glad that my personal life isn't as complicated as my work life!)

KEY STRATEGY #9
When using a folder/subfolder e-mail filing system, Keep it Simple (Stupid!)

Related to that, one overriding philosophy that I firmly believe in when creating a file folder structure for *any* of your e-mail systems is a critical philosophy that should also override almost everything you do in your e-mailing adventures (and in your entire life too!). This philosophy is called K.I.S.S., which stands for "Keep It Simple, Stupid." Obviously, you could go crazy having this capability to create folders, and folders inside of folders, and folders inside of folders inside of folders inside of folders, and on and on. You could conceivably have too much infrastructure—definitely more than you need.

Here's the problem with going too "deep" with your folder structure and making things too complex: you may actually get yourself to the point at which you effectively start to confuse yourself. Your system will become difficult and will thus take on a life of its own that is above and beyond what you're trying to do to be effective and productive. If your e-mail folder system becomes too complex, you'll actually start spending counterproductive time trying to both file and later find messages. The time and productivity gains you can receive by effectively filing your messages outside of your inbox will be lost if it takes you thirty seconds to a minute every time you have to file a message to move through several folders and subfolders to find the very specific subfolder where the e-mail belongs. Your productivity enhancement system will become a time stealer in and of itself.

I personally follow this general rule: I try to go no deeper than three levels in my e-mail account. I can have top-level folders, sublevel folders within the top-level folders, and one additional level of subfolders within subfolders. That's about the depth of the structure that I typically allow myself to have. I know from personal experience that if I start to go five, six, or seven levels deep, I'm potentially going to confuse myself and lose efficiency and productivity by making it hard both to file messages and later find them.

There is obviously a tradeoff here, and you need to figure out what is the right level of complexity or simplicity for you. Obviously, you want to have enough structure so that you have an appropriate place to file your messages so that you can quickly find them if you need them. But you don't want so much structure that the structure takes on that life of its own and starts to become counterproductive. The rule of three seems to have worked pretty nicely for me— effectively balancing my need for structure and also my need for efficiency, productivity, and speed—so that's the rule that I'm following. Figure out what is right for you.

E-mails with Split Personalities, and Losing E-mails in Your Filing Infrastructure

When I share this strategy in my live programs, some people immediately bring up this issue: "If I've got this folder structure, isn't it possible that some of my e-mails might 'belong' in more than one different folder? What do I do in that situation?" I always suggest that you put the e-mail in the most sensible folder. Yes, it is possible that the e-mail may be related to multiple clients, multiple projects, and/or multiple people, and it could thus go into several different folders. You have to ask yourself, "Which folder is the most intuitive and makes the most sense? Which folder is the one in which I'm most likely to look for this e-mail at a later date/time?" I certainly don't recommend you start making additional copies of a single e-mail message so you can put these copies in each additional folder. Once again, I think that is highly counterproductive. Try to simply put it in the most sensible folder.

At this point, some people will ask the obvious next question—"Isn't it then likely that I'll occasionally file a message and not be able to find it at a later date/time because I filed it in a folder other than the one that seems most obvious at that later time?" Yes, it is likely that you will do this occasionally. No system is perfect, and this is the single biggest "flaw" with the folder and filing structure system. But don't let that stop you from utilizing this system. My firm belief and practical experience is that the amount of time you save by not rereading completed messages over and over is significantly greater than the amount of time you'll spend occasionally searching for a message filed in the "wrong" folder. I have a very robust file structure system in my account—several hundred folders and subfolders, and I probably only have to do an intensive search for an e-mail about once every two or three weeks. Compare that to rereading "done" messages several times a day, and you can see how this system should save you significant time.

Related to this, a little later in the book in Chapter 11, you will learn a strategy related to how to use the search and sort tools in your e-mail software tool, especially within one of your other e-mail folders that we haven't discussed yet—the Sent folder—which should give you great confidence to follow this e-mail filing system. Some people resist because they're afraid they're not going to be able to find important messages later. The "search-and-sort" strategies shared later in the book should greatly relieve your fear of losing messages and give you absolute confidence in filing your messages appropriately. If you get into the habit of filing those messages, you're going to gain significant time and productivity, as long as the structure of your filing system makes sense to you.

The "Organic" File Structure System

Finally, I want to share with you another philosophy about how your e-mail file structure system should be developed. The philosophy is very simply this: think organic. My wife is a total believer in the organic food movement, and she wants to move us toward a point at which the vast majority of the foods we eat are grown naturally, without pesticides and chemical fertilizers, because they're much more healthy, have higher nutritional content, and probably will help us live a longer life. I like the organic philosophy when it comes to building your e-mail infrastructure also. When I say the "organic philosophy," what I mean is this: every single person should have a file system structure that is *natural* and *unique* to his or her professional and personal e-mail situation. In other words, you want to create a file structure—an organic file structure—that fits who you are as a person and who you are as a professional. It fits *your* circumstance and *your* needs.

Let me explain how this works by asking you a question: Guess how many file folders I had in my e-mail inbox the first day I started my time management and e-mail training and consulting business? How many folders and subfolders did

I have in that inbox folder on the very first day the business started? The answer, of course, is zero—all I had was my inbox.

Over time, I progressively followed the system I've been explaining in this chapter, and I created new folders when and as needed. Whenever I had an e-mail or a group of e-mails that needed to be filed, but didn't have a proper "home," I created the new folder(s) necessary to hold those messages in the moment the filing circumstance presented itself. Very often those folders started out as just simple top-level folders. "Oh, here are some e-mails from some prospective clients. I'm going to need a folder for "prospective clients." I would then create the "Prospective Client" folder.

Then I'd start filing e-mails into that folder, and then, after some more time, I'd start to realize, "Wow, I've got a lot of e-mails in here from a lot of different prospective clients. It's getting a little hard to find the specific messages from each individual prospective client. I had better start creating some subfolders within this folder for each of these specific prospective clients." So I'd do that. Then I would start to convert some of these prospective clients into real clients, and I'd realize that I needed a "Clients" folder in addition to my "Prospective Clients" folder. I would also need to move these specific prospective client subfolders from the "Prospective Clients" top-level folder up to the new top-level "Clients" folder, and so on and so forth.

By doing this, I slowly and progressively built an appropriate, reasonable, but not overly sophisticated file structure system. I've been doing this now for the 3+ years that I've been running my consulting and training business. I recently counted how many folders I have at the top level and every sublevel. I counted every single folder that I've created, and found that in about three years I've created more than 200 folders in my e-mail inbox. About 25 of those are top-level, and there are another 175 subfolders that drop down from those top-level folders—some at second level, some at third level, and there are one or two folders where I've actually gone four levels deep. As I mentioned earlier, I try to resist going too deep with my folder structure because I do not want to get to the point at which things are counterproductive.

I am a firm believer in the phrase "Rome was not built in a day." Another current-day information products and Internet guru, Alex Mandossian, shares a philosophy that says "Think progress, not perfection." You don't have to build the perfect file structure on Day One of following this system. What you want to do is make your best effort to build a decent structure starting out, and then continue improving and perfecting your file structure over the life cycle of your work and your e-mail account. If you do that in both your personal and your professional e-mail accounts, you'll be able to much better manage those accounts and use them efficiently and effectively as a powerful information archival and retrieval system. If you follow the philosophies shared in this chapter, you give yourself the opportunity to potentially be a highly effective and productive e-mail manager and professional.

Now let's move on to some specific strategies on getting your account to zero if you've got hundreds or even thousands of unfiled messages.

End of Chapter Review Questions:

- What is the key reason that you want to build a file "infrastructure" for your e-mail account?

- What does K.I.S.S. stand for? Why is it relevant when building and administering an e-mail filing infrastructure?

- How do you best handle e-mails that might have "split personalities"?

- What is a possible longer-term way to think about the development of your e-mail filing infrastructure?

Key Strategy Review:

Key Strategy #8: Create a personalized e-mail file folder infrastructure

Key Strategy #9: When using a folder/subfolder e-mail filing system, Keep it Simple (Stupid!)

Video Tutorials:

Video Tutorial #4: Creating a new electronic file folder in MS Outlook and Yahoo!(and moving messages from your inbox into an e-mail file folder).

PART II

**Getting to "Sanity" from a Mess:
How to Get Your Inbox to Zero**

CHAPTER 8

Cleanup Strategies for Those with 250 or Fewer "Legacy" E-mails

Up to this point, I've shared a number of strategies that will help you manage your e-mail account significantly better. All of these strategies will work even better if your account is not out of control when you start using them. You've probably been thinking, "Randy, these strategies are great—they're definitely going to help me—but what am I going to do with the existing 1,263 messages that are sitting in my inbox right now? Aren't they going to make it more difficult to follow these strategies? Do I just leave them there? Do I start using these strategies and just leave those "legacy" e-mails until some abstract time in the future?" Now is the time to learn how to get your old e-mails cleaned up and under control, so that you can truly get the most out of the strategies that I have shared up to this point.

Nearly everyone who is reading this book has an e-mail account that is anything but "clean." It's likely that you are starting with at least somewhat of a mess. What you need is a process to help you get your e-mail "beast" tamed and under control, and get all of your "legacy" e-mails properly sorted, filed, and/or deleted. In this and the next chapter, you're going to learn strategies for taking the legacy e-mails that have been just sitting there and getting those properly taken care of, so that you can feel total confidence in your e-mail management and administration activities.

This chapter provides strategies for those with 250 or fewer legacy e-mails cluttering up their e-mail inbox, while the next chapter shares a recommended process for those dealing with more than 250 messages, even up to thousands of messages. I do recommend that readers go through both chapters, as the strategies explained in both can be highly useful for regular e-mail management, regardless of the size of the mess you will be starting with in your inbox.

In essence, what I want to do is show you a system for getting your e-mail inbox completely cleared out—literally down to _zero_ messages—so that from this point forward you can manage your account with the goal of getting your e-mail inbox(es) down to zero at least once a week, if not every single day. Getting to zero every day is the stretch goal that I always tell people to go for. I do acknowledge the somewhat chaotic and crazy reality of many workplaces and homes, where getting to zero every day might be a bit much for a lot of people. That is why I believe a more realistic goal is to get to zero at least once a week.

KEY STRATEGY #10

Set a goal to get your professional e-mail account's inbox down to ZERO messages at least once per week.

That goal may be more reflective of our individual realities, but yet also indicates appropriate discipline, professionalism, and responsiveness when managing your e-mails. So let's move forward with the strategies you'll need to get your e-mail account fully under control if you have 250 or fewer messages.

First, I have a question for you: Did you create the file structure that I recommended back in Key Strategy #8 (Chapter 7)? Did you actually take the time to stop reading and create the file structure that we talked about—the "organic" and appropriate file structure that is relevant and specific to you and your personal work situation? If you haven't, then this is the first step you need to follow:

Step 1: Build Your E-mail Filing Infrastructure

Building this file structure in essence gives you the infrastructure that will allow you to quickly move and file messages—not just your new messages, but also the existing messages that have been cluttering up your e-mail inbox for some time. If you have not created your file structure, this is the time to do that. Stop reading this chapter, go back and follow all of the steps laid out in Key Strategy #8, and get your base filing infrastructure built. You're going to need this infrastructure if you want to quickly and somewhat painlessly clear out all of the existing old e-mails that have been haunting your inbox for some time now.

Stop now—build your file infrastructure!

Now on to the next step. The key thing you'll need to complete Step 2 is TIME.

Step 2: Block Designated Time on Your Calendar to File, Delete, and "Complete" E-mails

As you can probably guess, cleaning up your e-mail

account(s) is not a totally pain-free, exercise-free, and energy-free process. You need to actually commit to getting your inbox to zero this first time, and the first thing you need to do to meet this commitment is block some dedicated time on your calendar. If right now is not the best time (and what better time than the present?), you need to take a look at your calendar and find some designated available time for effective e-mail account administration and cleanup. If you've got 100 or more messages, I'd recommend blocking at least half a day, if not a full day. If blocking a half or full day is just not possible, could you divide up this project into two half-day sessions, or four two-hour sessions, or even an hour a day over the next week or two? I do recommend that you block the times for this process in close proximity to each other, because you'll want to keep your momentum once you get started.

Even if you have fewer than 100 messages to go through, I'd still recommend blocking at least half a day. And some of you with 500 or more messages may need more than a single day to complete this process (although in the next chapter, I'll share some recommendations on how you can speed this process up). Depending on the number of messages you are going through, and your personal speed at reviewing these messages and deciding on a proper action, you may or may not need this full amount of time. But you definitely need to block adequate time for this critical process. **So, stop reading, go to your calendar, and book some time for the cleanup.** If right now is not the designated time for the cleanup, you can put the book down and come back to it when you are actually ready to start.

*****

All right—are you ready to begin the actual process of cleaning up your e-mail account? If your e-mail inbox has anywhere from 10 e-mails all the way up to 250 messages, this is the process that I recommend you follow. If you have more than 250, keep reading the remainder of the recommendations in this chapter, but then go to the next chapter to get some additional time-saving strategies for cleaning up larger e-mail messes.

Step 3: One-by-One Review

If you have 250 or fewer messages, I typically recommend a one-by-one "review" process whereby you review each message—you actually go through and individually read each and every message.

As you read each message, you have a series of possible options, depending on the status of the e-mail.

"Completed" Messages. Completed messages are those for which you have already completed the defined action or task required by the e-mail. If the message is completed, you have one of two choices:

1. *If you don't need it, DELETE IT!* This is obviously rule number one for a reason—if you don't see a tangible reason for keeping the message, *get rid of it!* My hope is that you will simply delete a significant portion of the messages as you review them, thus reducing clutter and creating more space in your account. Many people will delete 30 to 50 percent or more of their legacy e-mails when following this process. (By the way, if you or your company faces any litigation risk at all, you might want to read the segment regarding litigation and e-mail in the next chapter before going "deletion crazy".)

2. *If you need it, and it is "completed," you MUST FILE IT.* Any message you have completed that has retention value, meaning you think you might need to reference it again in the future, should be filed appropriately in

one of the e-mail file folders you created as part of your e-mail file infrastructure. You need to file the old archival messages in a folder where everything has already been acted on, so you don't keep rereading them. It is obviously *a pure waste of time* to keep rereading a message you've already fully completed, and yet this is one of the most common time killers reported to me by many professionals frustrated with their e-mailing experience. By moving these completed e-mails out of your line of sight, you no longer will feel a need to review them just to make sure you've already gotten them done. Taking the few seconds to file the message in one of your other e-mail folders will save you hours of lost "review" time each year—and possibly each and every week!

a. *Now, here is a critical sub step:* If you have a completed e-mail that you want to keep for retention purposes, but you do not have a "natural" available folder to file this e-mail into, you need to *create a folder*, and then *file the message in that folder.* You need to do this *each and every time* you come across a "completed" e-mail that needs to be filed in an inbox subfolder.

During the first-pass effort at creating their e-mail infrastructure, many people take their best guess at the folders they need. Then they feel as if these folders are set in stone, and resist creating more folders. Completed messages thus continue to build up in the inbox, because there is no good place for them to go. *Get over this resistance!* You can keep creating and adding new folders whenever you need to, and this is *exactly* what you should do! If a message needs to be filed, and there is no natural folder for it to go into (including appropriate subfolders), then *create the folder!*

KEY STRATEGY #11

Get ruthless and quick at filing "completed" messages, and also at creating new folders for those messages if no good folder exists. (Corollary: Don't keep rereading completed messages!)

Make this a new e-mail "power habit," and get ruthlessly efficient at it. Make today the day that you stop rereading completed e-mails!

Active E-mails. Contrasted with "completed" e-mails, active e-mails are those for which there is still a defined task that you need to complete before you can either delete or file the message. There are three possible actions with these e-mails, depending on how much time it will take to complete the designated task(s) related to the e-mail:

1. *Three Minutes or Less—Complete the Task NOW!* As we mentioned earlier, every e-mail you receive that has a related task taking three minutes or less should be acted upon as soon as you decide to give your attention to that e-mail. Under no circumstances should that e-mail be allowed to just sit there to be done "later," because you'll likely reread it several times before taking the designated action, and thus spend three times as long completing the task as you would have had you just acted upon it when you first received it (see Chapter 3 as a reminder). Then, once the three-minute task is done and the e-mail moves from being an active e-mail to being a completed e-mail, file it or delete it as described in the previous section.

2. *Longer than Three Minutes—Task It or Print It.* If you read the message, and you determine that the defined

task(s) will take significantly longer than three minutes to complete, you have one of two choices:

a. ***Print It.*** You could simply print the e-mail message, and then create a "priority" pile of similar messages, with the most urgent/important message on top. Then, as you go through your workday, you will integrate these messages and their defined tasks into your work activities as appropriate.

b. ***Task It.*** Rather than printing the message, you could identify the affiliated task(s) from the message and add it/them to your task list, either in your PIM program (for example, MS Outlook) or in some paper format (notepad, planner). Then, once again, as you go through your workday, you will integrate these defined tasks into your work activities as appropriate according to their urgency and/or importance. (Note: this process was previously described in Chapter 4.)

Once you have either printed or tasked the message, it now can also be considered a "completed" message,* and then can be either deleted or filed, using the strategies described earlier for completed messages.

*Back in Chapter 4, I described the formation of a "Priority Processing" folder for your e-mail file infrastructure. The tasked or printed e-mails described here could also be filed in this Priority Processing folder following the strategy mentioned in that chapter. These messages are still somewhat "active" since the defined tasks have not actually been completed. You can then more quickly retrieve these e-mails if you need them for task completion. The important point is that once the task has been identified, or at least printed and prioritized, you should move that message out of your inbox so you once again can avoid rereading it until it is the right time to take appropriate action.

One final suggestion: If you blocked a whole day to get your e-mail cleaned up, and you've gone through all of these steps and now find yourself at only 2:30 p.m., don't get back to work quite yet. Instead, take your newly identified longer-than-three-minute tasks and/or printed e-mails and go through them to knock out any that are of the five- to ten-minute nature. You planned on burning a whole day to get your account under control and deal with a bunch of little stuff—why not make a whole day of it and really get rid of some e-mail volume? Then, you'll have a smaller task pile tomorrow, you'll feel more ready to attack the longer-form tasks and projects of higher importance and urgency, and you'll really be able to appreciate the proactive nature of this e-mail management system.

If you have 250 or fewer messages, and you follow the process explained in this chapter for all of your legacy e-mails—both active and completed—you'll probably find that it will take you about a day or less to go through all of your e-mails and get your inbox to zero. If you are not down to zero, you've not fully completed one of the steps. It's of interest that in my practical experience dealing with clients and course attendees who have used this process, 80 percent or more of the legacy e-mails most people are retaining in their inboxes will be properly removed from their e-mail inbox by using the three strategies of the Three-Minute Rule, simple deletion, and folder creation/appropriate filing.

Getting to "E-mail Zero"

So are you at zero? Did you get all the way there? Or did you skip or not fully complete one of the previously prescribed steps? (If so, go back and figure out where you missed something.)

If you are at zero now, how do you feel?

Most people who get to "e-mail zero" that first time report

a feeling of liberation and control that they haven't felt in some time. And, they now know it is actually possible to get to zero. If you can do it once, you now know you can do it over and over again. That builds confidence! Remember, now your goal is to get the e-mail inbox for your professional account to zero at least once a week, with a stretch goal of getting it to zero every single workday. *It is possible!* Make this your new reality from this point forward, and keep working your account from this new perspective.

Now, if you've got more than 250 legacy e-mails, and especially if you've got more than 500 or 1,000 messages, you might want to follow a slightly different process—which is outlined in the next chapter.

End of Chapter Review Questions:

- What is the first critical step necessary to start an effective e-mail cleanup process?

- What is the "pain" involved with an e-mail cleanup process?

- Once you complete your initial e-mail inbox cleanup process, what should now be your weekly goal related to your e-mail account?

- What is the difference between a "completed" e-mail and an "active" e-mail?

- Why is rereading "completed" e-mails so damaging to productivity?

- How do you convert an "active" e-mail into a "completed" e-mail?

Key Strategy Review:

Key Strategy #10: Set a goal to get your professional e-mail account's inbox down to ZERO messages at least once per week.

Key Strategy #11: Get ruthless and quick at filing "completed" messages, and also at creating new folders for those messages if no good folder exists. (Corollary: Don't keep rereading completed messages!)

CHAPTER 9

Cleanup Strategies for Those with More Than 250 "Legacy" E-mails

So, you've got more than 250 e-mails populating your inbox. I suspect that many of the readers of this book have significantly more than 250 e-mails. (If you are curious, at the time of writing, the largest number of legacy e-mails in a single person's e-mail inbox that I've come across is 14,000. That person actually knew he was going to meet me, so in the two days before meeting me, he went through his account and knocked it down to 8,000, and came in with a great amount of pride to tell me about his accomplishment. I let him know that even at 8,000, he still held the record!) And, of course, if you've got hundreds—or even thousands—of e-mails to go through, doing a one-by-one review as suggested in the previous chapter is simply not practical or workable. You might spend the next couple of months doing nothing but reviewing old e-mails, which in most organizations is likely to cause your dismissal!

You need some strategies to deal with this volume of messages with relative speed. What I want you to do is sacrifice a little bit of accuracy for speed, so that you don't spend a week (or month!) going through messages one by one and getting yourself totally behind the new work that's coming in. If you have hundreds or even thousands of legacy messages to review, I can see it being possible that the flow of new e-mail will be so fast that you'll never get caught up, and never get yourself to the point at which your account is actually "clean."

So, what do you do? In short, what I recommend is that you utilize some of the search and sort functions that exist in your e-mail tool to allow you to mass-delete and mass-file messages. This is a new key strategy:

KEY STRATEGY #12

When cleaning up hundreds or even thousands of legacy e-mails, sacrifice some accuracy for speed by using the "sort" function embedded in your e-mail software to mass-file and mass-delete messages.

Of course, this has a downside. It's likely that you will miss some latent, undone tasks by doing this—tasks or deliverables that you are probably responsible for but will never get to because you will file or delete the message with the embedded task without actually reading the message. But, you've probably been doing that anyway if you've got hundreds, if not thousands, of messages piled up in your inbox. At least now you should be able to get the account cleaned up and workable so that you will not miss any new tasks or deliverables moving forward.

Step 1: Create a "New E-mails" File Folder in Your Filing Infrastructure

To get ready for using the search and sort functions, the first step that I recommend you do is to create a "New E-mails" file folder in your e-mail filing infrastructure. If you have your e-mails already sorted by reverse chronological order (newest to oldest—the typical default setting in most commercial e-mail accounts), select and move the most recent e-mails from your inbox into this folder (for instance, all of the new e-mails you've received in the last two-to-three weeks). You will process these e-mails later, following the one-by-one strategy detailed in Chapter 8. By doing this, you will at least reduce the likelihood that you'll miss an important *new* task or deliverable request in your account.

For now, I want you to simply move these newer e-mails out of your inbox and into your "New E-mails" folder so they are out of the way for the next step in the process. This is easy to do—in Outlook, all you have to do is left-click on the first message you want to move, then hold down the "Shift" key, then left-click on the last message you want to move. This will select all of the messages that you want to move, and then you can left-click again on the selected messages and move them en masse by dragging and dropping them into your "New E-mails" file folder. This makes a great new video tutorial:

Video Tutorial #5: *How to mass-select groups of messages and move them into appropriate file folders, using left-clicks, the Shift key (and the "Ctrl" key for noncontiguous e-mails), and drag & drop.*

Remember to visit the Taming E-mail Reader web site at: http://www.tamingemailreader.com/videotutorials.html to see this and all of the other related video tutorials from *Taming the E-mail Beast.*

Remember this technique, as we will be using it several times in this chapter. Note: You can also move noncontiguous e-mails en masse by using the same process detailed here, but using the "Ctrl" key instead of the "Shift" key—another handy technique. *(To note: at the time of this writing, the tutorials provided are primarily demonstrations of Microsoft Outlook, the market-leading commercial e-mail program. We plan to post additional video tutorials over time for the other popular commercial e-mail programs. Check back often.)*

With your most recent e-mails out of the way, it is now time to begin handling the remaining legacy e-mails in your inbox.

Step 2: Use the "Sort" Function to Identify Message Groups that Can Be Filed or Deleted En Masse

Remember our initial discussion in this chapter—our goal here is relative *speed*. I want you to find groups of messages that can be moved or deleted en masse so you do not have to go through each and every one of your hundreds (or thousands!) of messages. Most popular commercial e-mail programs, such as MS Outlook, Lotus Notes, and GroupWise, allow you to sort messages using several variables, including sorting by date (the typical default setting), sorting by sender, and also sorting by subject. For example, when you are in the e-mail function in MS Outlook, you have the capability to sort messages by these variables in any e-mail folder.

You can actually "click" on any of the headers, including the "From" header, the "Subject" header, and/or the "Date" header, and you can sort by each of these fields almost like sorting in an MS Excel spreadsheet.

Click on any of these header bars to sort by that function (**Sender/ Recipient, Subject, Date Sent/Received, Size of Message**).

| Sender/ Recipient | Subject | Date Sent/ Received | Size of Message |

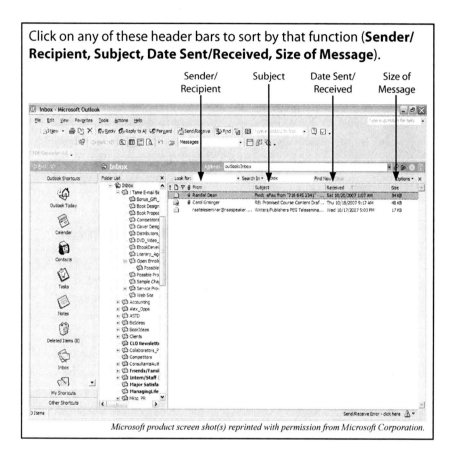

Microsoft product screen shot(s) reprinted with permission from Microsoft Corporation.

This is a perfect place for another video tutorial:

Video Tutorial #6: *How to sort messages by sender, subject, and/or date in MS Outlook, and also move those messages en masse.*

> **Remember to visit the Taming E-mail Reader web site at:**
> **http://www.tamingemailreader.com/videotutorials.html** to see
> this and all of the other related video tutorials from *Taming the
> E-mail Beast.*

If you just click on the "From" header, Outlook will sort your messages into alpha order by sender; if you click on the "Subject" header, it will sort your messages into alpha order by subject. As mentioned earlier, most e-mail systems are set up so that the default is to sort by date, giving you the newest to the oldest, but if you are in default mode and click on the "Date" header again, you can change the order so that it is sorted oldest to newest. All of this sorting capability creates some real power when it comes to quickly sorting and grouping messages and cleaning out your inbox.

Step 2A: Sort by Sender and Move En Masse

What I recommend at this point is to sort by sender. As we mentioned previously, what you are going to find is that all of the messages will be sorted in alpha order by person/e-mail address. Very often, when they're all sorted in that order, you can select a big group of messages all from the same person, and move the majority of those messages into one or two individual e-mail folders (using the strategy discussed earlier, by using either the "Shift" key if the messages are all next to each other, or the "Ctrl" key if the messages are close but not contiguous). You can move these selected messages out of your inbox and into the related appropriate project folder that would make sense for that person. Usually you can move these messages in large batches fairly quickly—for instance, a set of messages all from the same client or a set of messages all from the same vendor.

I recommend doing this sort "by person" first, because usually you'll look at the names of the senders and you'll quickly realize that "all of these messages from Joe Smith should go into this specific client folder," which is related to Joe Smith. Or they will go into a specific project folder that both you and Joe Smith are working on. Or, they may possibly go into a specific "Joe Smith" folder.

By sorting by person/e-mail address, you may also see a batch of messages coming from a certain sender that you realize you do not need at all. These messages could be mass-deleted by using the same selection process identified earlier and then hitting the "Delete" key (rather than dragging and dropping) once the messages are selected. Hopefully, the "by person" sort will allow you to quickly move and file—or delete!—a significant number of messages from different senders quite quickly. (Before you go "deletion crazy", you might want to read the *litigation segment* later in this chapter!)

Once you get all of the easily filed messages from specific people moved, you're likely to still have many messages left over. This leads to your next step.

Step 2B: Sort by Subject and Move Even More Messages En Masse

Your next step is to go in and sort by subject to see if there are certain messages that can also be moved in the same manner—multiple messages related to a specific subject (for instance, a project, client, or vendor) that can be moved en masse into a specified e-mail project or archival folder as recommended in Key Strategy #11, or possibly mass-deleted since you no longer need those e-mails. *One mini-strategy to consider:* If you sort by subject and find several messages with the same subject line, you have likely found an "e-mail string"—a string of messages all related to an original message sent sometime earlier. If many of these e-mails contain a string of text that is contained in all of the messages, you may only have to save one or two of the latest e-mails for your desired archival/retention purposes. The rest can be deleted, as they all have the same repetitive information.

After you go through the process of sorting and filing

messages by both person and by subject, you may still, depending on the number of messages in your inbox, have a good number of e-mail messages left to process. This leads to the next step:

Step 3: Sort by Date, and Either File or Delete the Oldest Messages Outright

The next step I recommend is this: consider the possibility of doing what I call "date-based deletion." Date-based deletion means that you take everything older than a certain date and make the "executive decision" that, because it is so old, you must not really need it any more. Typically, for many professionals, and depending on your line of business, the age of relevance for an e-mail is somewhere between six months and two years, with many professionals reporting that the one-year marker is a good one. Once an e-mail gets older than that, you can be pretty certain it has lost much of its retention value. This becomes even more apropos if you have already sorted by person and by subject as explained earlier—you've already screened, sorted, and filed the most important messages out of your account. If you've already sorted out the most important messages from your key people and your key subjects or projects, everything else that is left over must not be terribly important, and you can take the very limited risk of mass-deleting these leftover older messages. Before you start aggressively deleting all of these old e-mails, I do recommend that you check to see if there is an existing document/e-document retention policy already in place for your organization. Review that document and follow the policies already in place prior to deleting any messages, especially if there is any litigation risk in your work or line of business (more on this in just a moment).

If you are somewhat risk averse, and you are not sure if

there is an existing document retention policy in place, you could simply create a folder in your inbox titled "Old Unfiled E-mails," and then move all of these older leftover e-mails into this new folder, removing them from your line of sight in your inbox proper. If you do this, I recommend that you leave yourself a reminder to go back and empty this folder in another six to twelve months, especially if you've had no need to retrieve any information or messages from this folder, which is highly likely. (You could also follow the e-mail archiving tactics discussed in Chapter 12, so these e-mails are moved into your "personal folders" or other established e-mail archive and thus are removed from the active section of your e-mail account – a great strategy for reducing your e-mail accounts size and increasing its stability.)

Litigation Risk and E-mail Deletion vs. Retention

Do you have any litigation risk in your work or line of business? Do you ever correspond with individuals either internal or external to your firm regarding information, activities, or services where there is even only a small risk of a lawsuit? If you have any litigation risk in your business and/ or your work, you may want to think twice before deleting *any* messages. If you delete messages and you don't have a clear rationale as to why you deleted them, you could possibly run into some fairly serious legal issues and consequences.

Due to the actions of some fairly unscrupulous actors in the past, many courts have come to the point of suspecting wrongdoing when e-mails are deleted without a proper and documented rationale. In a litigation situation, you may be asked, "Why did you delete these e-mails? What was your purpose for deleting these e-mails?" If you can't explain it well, and you don't have documentation to support your reasoning, you may actually get yourself and your company into some significant legal trouble. (Another good reason to have formal document retention policies! More on this shortly.) Thus, I want you to keep any and all messages that may have any relation to potentially litigious matters, regardless of how hard your IT group is pressuring you to delete your old e-mails.

Let IT know that before you can delete these specified e-mails that you need to either refer to your organization's formal document retention policy or consult with the company's legal staff/counsel.

If you do not have a formal document/e-document retention policy to follow, and you do decide to seek legal counsel, let them know that you would like to clean up space in your e-mail account and get it under control. Explain that you are trying to follow a new regimen that will allow you to be much more on top of your e-mail system, but that you wanted to consult with them first regarding any possible litigation risk related to the deletion of e-mail documents. If your legal department says, "Yes, there is litigation risk" and they advise you to not delete any e-mails, *please* heed their advice. Here is my recommendation if your legal department requests for you to not delete e-mails prior to the development of a formal document/e-document retention policy:

Create a folder within your inbox structure, like the one we explained briefly earlier, and call it "Old E-mails Before _____," using the date of your file cleanup. Suppose you had decided that everything more than a year old is going to be targeted for deletion. Instead of deleting those messages, select all of them and, en masse, drop them into that "Old E-mails Before _____" folder. This way, they'll be out of your inbox proper (and thus out of your line of sight), but you'll have that folder to cover your litigation risk. (By the way, if you jump ahead to Chapter 12 and read the information on archiving your e-mails outside of your active e-mail account, you might be able to avoid deleting any potentially litigious messages by instead placing them in a working e-mail archive. Consult with your IT staff on proper archiving procedures.)

Formal Document and E-Document Retention Policies and IT vs. Legal

Now some people are probably saying, "Hearing about this litigation risk, why would you ever delete any potentially litigious e-mails? Why not just file them in an 'old e-mails' folder or an appropriate e-mail archive?" A good question with a simple answer – if there is a litigation risk, then the e-mail should be kept unless there is a formal document and/ or e-document retention policy in place that makes very clear when it is OK or not OK to delete e-mails.

Now, of course, your IT staff might prefer for you to delete messages whenever you possibly can. Why? It frees up space and memory, both in your e-mail account and on your hard drive or your share drive. It thus reduces the load on your e-mail and storage systems and servers. In addition, your IT support staff is probably going to like you for being diligent and disciplined with your e-mail account and your company's electronic storage capacity. But your IT staff's desire for a lower memory load on the corporate e-mail and document servers should never override proper legal document retention standards. Here's a key question: What is of higher importance—space and memory usage, or litigation risk? If managing the risk of future litigation is more important, you probably want to save the e-mails. If cleaning out space is of utmost importance and litigation risk is relatively small or nonexistent, then you might want to delete those messages.

But if you want to help yourself and your team feel more confident with what you can or must keep and what you can or must delete, then follow the next key strategy:

KEY STRATEGY #13

Learn what your company's formal document and e-document (including e-mail) retention policies are, and follow them. If they do not exist, press your legal staff/counsel to research and develop appropriate policies for your organization.

One reason people might be keeping too many e-mails is that they don't know what they should keep or what they should delete. They have some undefined fear of deleting something that might be needed later, including those messages that may be requested in a future litigation situation. With formal document/e-document retention policies in place (and well understood by the professional staff in your company), people can act with greater confidence when it comes to keeping and deleting documents and e-documents, including e-mails.

I strongly believe your company's legal staff and/or counsel should be the group that researches and writes the document and/e-mail retention policies in companies (possibly in consultation with the IT staff.) The legal staff should have a much better feel for where litigation risk exists and what standards need to be applied and followed. IT tends to be more arbitrary, and makes these decisions from an "operating cost" perspective—"Because of cost, you can only have 'X' amount of space. If you exceed your allotted memory, you will get warnings to delete unnecessary e-mails." Of course, if you are deleting e-mails with significant litigation risk simply because "IT told me so," that may fly about as far as you will in a courtroom situation.

Make sure the right people in your company are weighing in on these decisions and are providing appropriate guidance for the development and use of these policies. Everything I've seen says that "appropriate guidance" is a written, specific, *customized*, and formal "Document and E-mail/Electronic File Retention Policy" that is developed by your company's legal staff and/or advisers, with input by your IT department and senior management. (When I say customized, that means you don't just pull some form document off the web and state that it is your new document retention policy – it must be specific and appropriate for your company and your company's market and litigation risk situations.)

If you do have a formal retention policy, and it clearly states that all e-mails older than a year are to be deleted, then make this the first step of your cleanup process, rather than Step 3! Sort by date, and delete everything older than a year in your inbox. Your document retention policy gives the right to do that, so go for it! Then, follow Step 1 and Step 2 in this chapter for all the e-mails that remain.

*****

So, this is the recommended three-step process that you need to follow when you've got hundreds or even thousands of messages to go through, notwithstanding my little "sidetrack" on legal matters. We're nearly done, and most of the heavy lifting should be complete (meaning you've effectively moved a good number of your e-mails from your inbox). Now, what to do with the messages that remain?

Step 4: Move the Messages in Your "New E-mails" Folder BACK into Your Inbox

Do you remember the "New E-mails" folder I had you create earlier in the chapter, and that you populated with the newer e-mails you've received in the last two to three weeks? Yes, I want you to take those messages and move them back into your inbox, so they can be rejoined with any of the remaining messages that you did not move/file or delete following the "sort by sender/subject/date" process detailed earlier. You want to get all of your current, active e-mails back into your inbox for proper processing.

Step 5: Take These Remaining Messages, and Follow the Process Recommended in Chapter 8 *to the Word.*

You've taken out the bulk, and only the "cream" remains. Chapter 8 lays out exactly how to deal with all of these remaining e-mails on a one-by-one basis, and now is the time to do just that. After following the sorting and moving/filing/ deleting steps laid out earlier in this chapter, you should be dealing with a much more reasonable number of messages—a number of messages that can be reviewed on a one-by-one basis throughout the rest of this designated e-mail cleanup day. You also should be rapidly approaching the "zero inbox" we discussed in great detail in Chapter 8. Keep going after it—you can, should, and *will* get to zero if you follow this process, and then you can once again own your e-mail account rather than it owning you!

End of Chapter Review Questions:

- What is it that you have to sacrifice in order to clean up hundreds or even thousands of inbox messages in a reasonably quick and efficient manner?

- What embedded tool in most commercial e-mail software programs helps to facilitate an efficient clean-up process?

- What is the recommended thing to do with old e-mails – especially those with potential litigation risk – in the absence of a formal document retention policy?

- Why is a formal document/e-document retention policy so helpful for keeping individual e-mail accounts clean?

- Who should be responsible for developing your company's formal document/e-document retention policy? Why?

Key Strategy Review:

Key Strategy #12: When cleaning up hundreds or even thousands of legacy e-mails, sacrifice some accuracy for speed by using the "sort" function embedded in your e-mail software to mass-file and mass-delete messages.

Key Strategy #13: Learn what your company's formal document and e-document (including e-mail) retention policies are, and follow them. If they do not exist, press your legal staff/counsel to research and develop appropriate policies for your organization.

Video Tutorials:

Video Tutorial #5: How to mass-select groups of messages and move them into appropriate file folders, using left-clicks, the Shift key (and the "Ctrl" key for noncontiguous e-mails), and drag & drop.

Video Tutorial #6: How to sort messages by sender, subject, and/or date in MS Outlook.

CHAPTER 10

Once You've Got It Clean, Don't Lose Control!

If you followed the strategies suggested in the previous two chapters, you should have an e-mail account that is once again "clean"—meaning it is back down to zero messages, or at least very close to zero. This leads into learning how to keep it that way.

KEY STRATEGY #14
Once You Get Your E-mail Account Clean, Don't EVER Let It Get Re-cluttered and Disorganized

Keep that e-mail account under control. Once you find your e-mail sanity, don't allow yourself to lose it. Once your e-mail beast is finally tamed, don't let it go wild again. Now is the time to maintain your discipline and follow the many strategies that you learned in earlier chapters about how to effectively manage the new e-mails coming into your account. You want to give yourself the opportunity to keep your account close to zero on a regular, daily basis, and you should be able to do that if you follow the prescribed strategies shared earlier in the book, especially the Three-Minute Rule; keeping only active items in your inbox; printing or tasking e-mails; adding new folders when needed; and using a "Priority Processing" folder in your e-mail account.

If you have cleaned out all of the old e-mails according to the strategies in Chapters 8 and 9, and you have built your file infrastructure appropriately, there is no reason that you should not be able to keep up with your e-mail account on a regular, daily basis. The only reasons that should cause you to lose control are 1) that you stop following the earlier strategies, or 2) that you simply receive way too many e-mails on a daily basis, and you cannot possibly keep up (reread Chapter 1 about "Knowing Your E-mail Flow").

If you have followed all of these strategies but still can't keep up with the flow of your e-mail—if you find yourself slipping back down the "cluttered" path—this may indicate a potential job design issue. In other words, there are so many messages coming in that a single person can't keep up with the volume. If this is the case, it is time to have a conversation with your superiors regarding job design and resources. You probably need help and additional support to properly manage the amount of work your e-mail is creating. Let your supervisor know that you've followed the strategies in this book to a T, and you still haven't solved your e-mail flow issue. (By the way, later in the book, we briefly talk about some e-mail automation options including web- and software-based solutions for mitigating excessive e-mail flow.) When your supervisor sees everything you've done up to this point, he or she may be more likely to support your request for additional resources, whatever those resources might be.

At this point I'm going to assume that you now can actually keep up with the flow of e-mails and related tasks, since you have your e-mail infrastructure built and your new e-mail management habits in place. Here's what you have to do now: *Keep up with it.* It's that simple. *Keep up with it.* Don't let your e-mail account slip! Don't let your e-mail beast loose!

Here's how I guarantee that I will never let my account get out of control again:

KEY STRATEGY #15

Set a Personal Maximum to the Number of E-mails You Will Allow to Gather in Your Professional Account

Following this Key Strategy means that with my primary professional e-mail account, I set a maximum number of e-mails that I will allow to "gather" in my account, and if it reaches that number, my e-mail suddenly becomes Priority #1. All other tasks, responsibilities, and deliverables become subjugated in priority to my e-mail. And I will keep working on my e-mail until I get it down to less than half of my maximum.

For me, I've set the maximum for my professional e-mail account to twenty messages. Once my inbox reaches twenty messages, I have to stop working on other things and process my e-mails using the system shared thus far until I get that e-mail account back under ten messages. Processing my e-mail becomes the most important thing I have to work on until I get my inbox back down under ten messages (and ideally down to zero messages!) Then I can go back into my usual mode of operation. I don't ever want my inbox to go above twenty messages, because I have determined that twenty messages is the beginning of the "slippery slope." If my inbox gets up above twenty messages, I've got a major concern—a concern that I'm about to lose control of my e-mail—and I don't ever want to let that happen.

Some of you, according to your flow of incoming messages, might be saying, "My e-mail gets to twenty new messages several times per day. Does this mean that several times per day I have to stop working on my other work, drop everything, and put my full focus on my e-mail?" In short, YES! This is fully consistent with the earlier discussions in the book. Remember that I recommended for you to check your e-mail only three to five times per day to avoid the bad behavior of "blinging", and to allow you to have buckets of time for dedicated single-tasking. If you check your messages in these dedicated times, and you find that your inbox gets over twenty messages, just follow the prescribed processes and strategies described earlier in this book. That should allow you to get your e-mail down to near zero *every single time* you process your e-mails.

Now, I certainly *do not* want you to be constantly monitoring your e-mail to see if it has reached that twenty-message threshold. If you are doing that, you are in essence blinging. Instead, trust and accept that messages will continue to come in while you are working on your individual tasks and projects, with your full focus and effort, in single-tasking mode. Then, when you hit your e-mail windows, you will then give your full effort, attention, and energy to getting your inbox back under control. It is perfectly consistent with the philosophy of this book for your e-mail to become Priority #1 a few times per day, but then for it to also completely disappear from your focus several times per day. This is exactly how I want you to manage your account.

From a bigger-picture perspective, I look at e-mail account management this way—it is just like getting yourself back in shape. If you've ever let yourself slack off on your fitness routine, you know it is a lot of work to get back into form. But if you've ever done this, you also know that it is much easier to stay in shape once you are there. It just requires an appropriate maintenance program. The same can be said for your e-mail. If you've made all of this effort to get your e-mail account back in shape—to get your e-mail beast tamed—don't let it slip. If you follow the prescribed strategies and techniques for new messages shared in this book, you have in essence found your appropriate maintenance program, and you should actually be able to keep your e-mail account in good shape from this point forward. Just keep your positive new habits! (I don't know about you, but I suddenly feel motivated to start a rigorous workout program again!)

I've been following these strategies—more or less—for the better part of ten years now. That means ten years of keeping my professional e-mail account to twenty messages or less on a regular daily basis, and very often getting my inbox to zero (usually once a week or more). It is possible. I'm living proof of it, as are several of the people who have attended my e-mail management courses in the past. If you can get yourself to follow these strategies, you can make this your e-mail reality.

You Can Be A Bit More Flexible With Your Personal Account.

Now, with my personal e-mail account, I'm not quite as "tight." There are times when that account will go up as high as fifty or even 100 messages. That is because these messages typically are not that urgent in nature (I'll even take messages that are more "professional" in nature that appear in my personal account and forward them to my professional account, so they get processed using the more rigorous system prescribed in this book). My personal account is more of a fun account, so I don't administer it quite as tightly—25 to 50 messages on a normal daily basis. Every month or so I'll go in and purge a bunch of these personal e-mails, file a bunch of e-mails into their proper folders, and try to get the inbox back down well below twenty, but I don't stress about the administration of that account – I manage it a little bit looser. (I usually only get it down to zero maybe once or twice a year – a great "to do" for over the holidays!) Contrast that with my professional e-mail account—that's the one I keep under tight control, because that way I know that I'm on top of things concerning my work and its related e-mail.

This is the philosophy toward effective e-mail management that I recommend. Don't forget that stretch goal we mentioned earlier—to get your e-mail down to *zero* every single day. But I also realize that goal is not necessarily realistic for everybody every single day because of the flow of work you have, the unexpected interruptions and changes of plans, the projects and tasks on tight deadlines that you are working on, and the number of meetings that you are in on any given day. Because of all of these things, it simply may not be possible to get your professional e-mail to zero every single day (but that doesn't mean you can't try!)

Within Striking Distance of Zero.

If you follow this system for daily e-mail management— and your work is not completely insane—you should have an excellent chance to get your professional e-mail account down to zero at least once a week. That is the more realistic goal I recommend for most professionals administering their professional accounts. If you know you're getting it down to zero at least once a week, and you're within "striking distance" of zero on any given day, that takes away a lot of the stress that your e-mail account may be bringing into your work and life. You know you are on top of it, more or less. And that makes your e-mail one less thing you have to worry about, thus giving you the possibility of directing your energy and focus to the bigger and more important areas of opportunity in your work and life. Maybe the next items you'll attack are the loose papers in your office, as we discussed a little bit earlier in the book. Then you'll get your garage clean, position yourself better for that next promotion at work, write the next Great American Novel, and take your snorkeling trip to the Great Barrier Reef. In the bigger scheme of things, getting your e-mail under control is obviously a relatively small accomplishment, but it certainly could be the springboard to other bigger and better personal and professional aspirations.

This is of course what I want you to do—I want you to turn your e-mail back into a proactive tool for continuous performance that allows you to achieve bigger things, versus being a reactive tool that is creating a lot of unnecessary stress and urgency (and thus sapping your energy and motivation.) Follow these strategies and get yourself there. If you do, you're going to give yourself a great opportunity to feel good about where you're at with your e-mail account, and possibly with your life!

Now, let's change our focus a bit, and talk about some of the additional capabilities of your e-mail, as well as a completely contrarian theory about filing your e-mail messages that you should at least consider.

End of Chapter Review Questions:

- Why is it important to keep your professional e-mail account "under control" once you've taken the effort to get it to "zero"?

- When does your professional e-mail account become "Priority #1" on your daily to-do list?

- Why is it more important to manage your professional e-mail account more "tightly" than your personal account?

Key Strategy Review:

Key Strategy #14: Once you get your e-mail account clean, don't EVER let it get re-cluttered and disorganized

Key Strategy #15: Set a personal maximum to the number of e-mails you will allow to gather in your professional account

CHAPTER 11

File *Nothing*?
And a Quick Discussion on
Searching and Sorting

U p to this point in the book, I've been a very strong
advocate of filing every single message that you
determine has retention value. You file the message once the
designated action related to the message has been taken or the
designated task at least has been identified and properly added
to your task list. My premise has been simply this—you don't
want those messages sitting in your inbox if you've already
taken the action or determined the task, because if they are
sitting there, you are very likely going to look at them over
and over and over again. And every time you look at them,
trying to figure out whether you've actually done the thing
that needs to be done, you're wasting time. I believe this is
a valid premise for most people, including me personally, as
well as likely for you too!

However, there is an alternate e-mail management theory
out there—a theory that says "File Nothing"—that I think is
important to share. I like to share this alternate theory because
I actually think there is a part of it that is very, very useful
when it comes to e-mail management. If you use this strategy,

it may allow you to feel even more confident about moving forward and *filing all of your messages* (which is sort of ironic, eh?)

File Nothing?

Here's what the alternate theory basically says: Why bother filing your e-mail at all? Why bother with spending all of this time creating folders and moving messages? Why not just use the search and sort functions that are embedded within your e-mail account to go back and find any message that you want when you need it? This is the counter-theory that flies in the face of everything I've espoused thus far. I don't fully subscribe to it, simply because I believe that messages gathered in your inbox provide a great distraction, and that most people will gain time by creating folders and filing messages. I know, however, that some people may challenge me on this. They may believe that the "over/under" (time saved vs. lost) on creating files and moving messages isn't worth the effort; thus, these users will support this counter-theory. If you have a really strong will, are very disciplined, and have an excellent memory, perhaps this alternate strategy will work for you. But, if you are like me and most other people, my bet is that you will lose time by using this "no filing" strategy. Test it out and let me know!

This is a theory that I believe was originally espoused by the Google guys—the people who developed Google's Internet-based e-mail service, Gmail. When they developed this tool, they recommended a philosophy of "don't file anything." I can picture them saying, "We're going to give you 2 gigabytes (GB) of storage for your e-mail [truly a massive amount of storage!] You can save years' worth of e-mail with 2GB of storage, and that is exactly what we want you to do. We want you to save all of your e-mails, because by doing

115

this, we can then use the text from your e-mails—both sent and received—to scan your e-mail text and provide you with defined, related search results." This is exactly what Google is doing, which is both quite interesting and something you need to know when you sign up for Gmail. Basically, Google is scanning the text in your e-mails using its search spiders and then providing you with search-related advertising that gives you links so you can find out more about the subjects and topics contained within your e-mails.

Now, for some people, that's downright spooky and reeks of "Big Brother." Those Google servers are basically checking out what you are doing in your e-mail every day. For others, this targeted text-based search is very handy. Let's say you have a passion for windsurfing, and you are sending a lot of e-mails back and forth with your windsurfing buddies. Google will see that you're having a lot of discussions on windsurfing and related activities, and will provide you with search links so that you can get even more good information about windsurfing. You personally might find having those search results quite handy. (Thus, it might make a lot of sense to consider Gmail for a personal account if you discuss many of your personal passions with family and friends.)

As I mentioned earlier, these contrarians believe that you do not need to sort and file your messages into folders. There is a nugget of brilliance here: the idea of using your search and sort functions to find messages. I'm a pragmatist—I like to use what works—and this recommendation to use your search and sort tools is a very good recommendation. In fact, it may actually give you more confidence to go ahead and file your messages into appropriate file folders.

Knowing How to Use Search and Sort Creates Confidence in Filing.

How can you use search and sort functions to be more confident in filing your e-mails? Here's how I do it: when e-mails arrive in my inbox, I follow my system and aggressively file or delete messages once they're completed or tasked. But I take a very different tack with e-mails that I send. Instead of filing these "sent messages", I basically just leave the vast majority of them sitting in my "Sent Items" folder. I keep as many as I can keep in there. Here's why: think about the messages that you receive in your primary e-mail account, especially those messages that have real work value (not junk or spam). What percentage of those e-mails do you estimate that you actually reply to, carbon copy (CC) someone, or forward on to somebody else? When I present my programs—all around the United States and abroad—I ask that question. The vast majority of people in these programs estimate that they typically reply to, CC, or forward anywhere from 60 to 90 percent of the "real e-mails" they receive.

Do you know what that means? That means that your "Sent Items" folder is, in essence, a surrogate for what your e-mail inbox would be if you weren't deleting or filing messages from it. In other words, it's a ghost or a mirror of your inbox—an approximate copy of what your inbox would be if you filed nothing—and this is extremely useful.

Here's why it's useful: Not filing anything in this folder allows you to use the sort functions that we discussed in Chapter 9—back when I talked about the way to properly clean out your account—to also help you find any needed messages that you may have filed in a folder that is no longer obvious to you. As I mentioned earlier, building a robust file structure makes it likely that you will "misplace" a message every once in a while. Occasionally you will place a message in a folder and then have difficulty finding it at a later date; you may put it in a folder that makes sense at the time, but may not be fully intuitive when you go back to find it. This may make you less trusting of the "file everything" strategy. But, if you've got any replies or forwards of that message still in your "Sent Items" folder, you can use the sort functions discussed previously, as well as the search function to find the message.

Using Search

Many commercial e-mail programs offer very robust search options. In MS Outlook, you can enter just about any string of text in the search field (in other words, you can search by the name of the person sent to or received from, search by the subject of the message, and even search for specific text you know is mentioned within the body of the e-mail).

Location of the Search Tool in MS Outlook
– simply click on the "Find" button and then enter your search term(s) in the "Look for:" field.

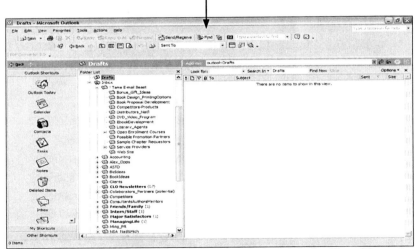

Microsoft product screen shot(s) reprinted with permission from Microsoft Corporation.

The e-mail search tool will scan the specified mail folders, giving you a great opportunity to find the message that you may have misplaced when using your inbox filing strategy. The default in MS Outlook is to scan not only the sender field and the subject field, but also the body text of the message, although under "Options" near the search tab/feature, you can de-select the body text scanning option.

KEY STRATEGY #16
Learn how to use your e-mail system's embedded "Search" tool.

If you are going to be filing all of your retained messages moving forward, you definitely want to learn how to effectively use both the search and the sort functions in your e-mail software programs. Becoming efficient at sorting and searching will give you even greater confidence in filing your "completed and needed" messages in your inbox, because you will know that in a relatively quick and painless manner, you can retrieve any message that you've kept and filed.

This obviously is a perfect opportunity for a video tutorial:

Video Tutorial #7: *Using the e-mail "Search" tool to find a missing message.*

Remember to visit the Taming E-mail Reader web site at: http://www.tamingemailreader.com/videotutorials.html to see this and all of the other related video tutorials from *Taming the E-mail Beast.*

Once again, here's the basic premise of the strategy detailed in this chapter: Use your "Sent Items" folder to help you find any messages that you may have misplaced by using the "sorting" strategy previously discussed in Chapter 9. Also, learn how to use your e-mail's search capabilities as well, so you have yet another tool for finding a misplaced message.

As I said earlier, I'm a pragmatist and I like to use what works – by using the "Sent Items" folder to help me find any misplaced messages (which I do fairly frequently) as well as using the search capabilities embedded within my e-mail programs, I am much more confident about moving my completed messages. I want you to be a pragmatist too, and learn how to use these valuable functions and capabilities. Happy sorting and searching!

End of Chapter Review Questions:

- What is the rationale behind the "File Nothing" e-mail management counter theory?

- How can this theory actually help you be more confident when filing your e-mail messages?

- Why do I file virtually nothing in my Sent Items folder?

- What two embedded tools in your e-mail software are most helpful for finding misplaced messages?

Key Strategy Review:

Key Strategy #16: Learn how to use your e-mail system's embedded "Search" tool.

Video Tutorials:

Video Tutorial #7: *Using the e-mail "Search" tool to find a missing message.*

CHAPTER 12

Using Your E-mail's Archiving Function for Better Speed and Stability

In recent chapters, we've discussed how to set up an organic folder structure within your e-mail's inbox, and also how to then move messages that you want to keep for retention purposes into inbox subfolders, but no longer want to keep in your inbox proper. This way, you'll have messages filed in appropriate e-mail file folders for easy access, while also helping to keep your e-mail inbox clear of completed or tasked messages. It is a very sensible system, and one that will allow you to keep critical focus and efficiency when administering new messages that you receive.

One final suggestion for you related to e-mail filing and retention is that you learn how to use your e-mail's "archive" function. Many commercial e-mail products allow you to archive older messages so they no longer reside in the active segment of your e-mail account. This is beneficial because filing messages into your e-mail's archive reduces the working size of your active e-mail account. Older messages moved into the archive function no longer reside in the active memory of your live account—instead, they are moved onto either your hard drive or your defined share drive or back-up drive, as determined by your company's IT staff. Having your e-mail at a smaller total size benefits you in two ways:

1. **Your e-mail account will operate faster and with more efficiency.** It won't be as slow or "clunky" as it might be right now. With fewer items taking up space in the active memory of your program, the program will work more quickly. You will be able to find newer messages more quickly, with your search and sort functions working faster.

2. **Your e-mail account/program will also be more stable.** My understanding is that most e-mail programs have a functional memory limit, and that when your e-mail account approaches this memory limit, instabilities may occur. The program may start working less efficiently, you might start having program and system errors, and it is even conceivable that the program will completely stop working. You might also lose messages/files residing in your e-mail program if you pass the functional memory buffer. Obviously, because e-mail (and affiliated PIM program features) are very critical assets for most working professionals, any instability or downtime is a major cause for concern. Moving old e-mails (and old calendar entries, completed tasks, and so on) to your archive will help to better stabilize your e-mail program by allowing it to operate within its normal performance and memory parameters.

So, it makes sense to learn how to utilize this valuable function within your e-mail program, leading to the next key strategy.

KEY STRATEGY #17

Learn How to Properly Set Up and Use Your Primary E-mail's Archival Function

Typically, an archival function within an e-mail program allows you to set up individual back-up folders within an archival folder. These back-up folders should parallel the folders that are both standard within your account (such as inbox, deleted items, and sent items), as well as the new folders you've created within your e-mail inbox per the earlier suggestions in this book (clients, customers, vendors, and so on).

The archival tool will also provide you with an option to set up the properties of the archival function, which may include setting up the parameters of auto-archiving. Auto-archiving sets the terms for how often your e-mail program goes through old e-mails (and other PIM files/items, such as tasks and calendar items) and moves them from your active files to your archive files. It may also give you the opportunity to simply auto-delete e-mails and other files within some folders after a certain amount of time.

Within Microsoft Outlook, you can set the parameters of the auto-archive, meaning you can set how often your auto-archive function runs to move old e-mails out of the active program into the archive (every seven days, fourteen days, twenty-eight days), as well as defining at what age e-mails should be moved (for example, after an e-mail is three months, six months, or twelve months old). Thus, you can set the terms for how often messages are moved or deleted, as well as how old messages must be before they are moved or deleted.

Creating an Archive Folder in Microsoft Outlook

Here is the process to follow to establish an archive folder for an existing folder or subfolder in your MS Outlook:

1. Single "Left Click" any existing folder for which you would like to create an archive file, to select that folder.
2. Right click on the selected folder. This makes a drop-down menu appear with several options. Scroll down and select "Properties".
3. Click the "Auto Archive" tab in the Properties window. This will provide you with a series of archiving options, including options for using the default archive settings and also auto-deleting old messages. I recommend that you ...
4. Select the "Archive this Folder Using These Settings" button, and then set the age at which old items get moved from your active to your archive folder (3 months, 6 months, 12 months, and so on – you make the decision according to what is appropriate for your line of business.)
5. Then, select the "Move Old Items to the Default Archive Folder" button. This step will create an automatic, "parallel" folder in your e-mail archive with the same name and location as the folder or subfolder in your active inbox.
6. Finally, click the "Apply" button, and then hit the "OK" button to close the Properties box.

Following this process will allow you to build an archive within your Microsoft Outlook, located in the "Archive Folders" section of your Folder List. When your auto-archive function runs within your e-mail, this new archive folder will automatically be created, and any e-mails now older than your designated archive setting will be moved from your active folders to your archive folders.

This leads to yet another Key Strategy:

KEY STRATEGY #18

Consider setting up the auto archive properties immediately upon the creation of any new folder or subfolder.

Following this strategy every time you create a new folder in your active e-mail account will help you take the thinking out of building a robust and workable archive for your e-mails. It will simply happen automatically every time your auto-archive tool runs in your e-mail, and help to keep your e-mail account's memory load manageable and stability more reliable. Your e-mail will work better, and your IT staff won't harass you about the size of your e-mail account (a little more information on archiving and your IT staff is coming shortly – keep reading!)

Setting up the archival folders and properties is actually quite easy within Microsoft Outlook, but it is not terribly easy to describe in text, so I have created a video tutorial on how to do these things:

Video Tutorial #8: *Setting up your Auto Archive general settings, and also your Auto Archive properties for individual folders within your e-mail inbox structure.*

Remember to visit the Taming E-mail Reader web site at: http://www.tamingemailreader.com/videotutorials.html to see this and all of the other related video tutorials from *Taming the E-mail Beast.*

In this video tutorial, I show you both how to set the general properties of your "auto archive" function, as well as how to make sure the properties are properly set for each of your individual e-mail inbox folders. Then, whenever your auto archive function runs, you'll know that many messages are being automatically moved from your live account to your archive, thus increasing the speed and stability of your live e-mail while also reducing the active size of the e-mail.

Ideally, if you set up your archive properly, you will have a functional copy of the files and folders in your working e-mail account. Thus, if you ever need to find an old message, it should be as easy as finding a new message. Instead of going into your active working files, you instead go into your archive folder list, find the parallel folder in your archive, and find the old message that you need. Now, if you don't properly set up your archive with similar parallel structure, then finding your e-mails may be more challenging. Thus, before creating your e-mail archive I recommend the following suggestion:

Consult with Your IT Staff Before Creating/Modifying Your E-mail Archive. While creating an archive and setting your properties is a relatively easy thing to do as an individual user, if you are working in a large group/organizational/ corporate setting, I do strongly recommend that you at least consult with your IT staff before creating/adjusting the settings of your e-mail program's archive. Your IT staff may already be following defined corporate/IT policies regarding the administration and proper back up of your e-mail files. Additionally, they may have a defined share drive or back up drive that they prefer these archives to save to. If you decide to personally go in and change these settings, you might affect or modify pre-set internal properties that may actually increase the likelihood that you'll lose valuable data or old e-mails, not only for yourself, but for many other users in your organization. And, you might just upset your IT staff in the process (never a wise thing to do!) You may even want to request that the IT staff hold a training program or at least put out a "best practices" paper on how to set up and properly use the e-mail archival function within your corporate setting (this would also be a great time to once again review your corporate/ organizational document/e-document retention policies!) By following the IT group's instructions, you will get all of the benefits of having a functional archive, and yet still work within proper organizational IT rules and parameters. And, your e-mail account will be stable, work faster, and you'll stop getting those annoying "Too many messages in your account" notices.

Enjoy setting up your archive, and using a more stable, robust, and speedy e-mail program!

End of Chapter Review Questions:

- What are the two key reasons for setting up and using an e-mail archive?

- When is the very best time to set up the auto-archiving properties for any of your folders in your active e-mail account?

- In a corporate/organizational setting, why is it important to consult with your IT staff prior to creating and using an e-mail archive?

Key Strategy Review:

Key Strategy #17: Learn how to properly set up and use your primary e-mail's archival function.

Key Strategy #18: Consider setting up the auto archive properties immediately upon the creation of any new folder or subfolder.

Video Tutorials:

Video Tutorial #8: Setting up your Auto Archive general settings, and also your Auto Archive properties for individual folders within your e-mail inbox structure.

PART III

Carbon Copies, Forwards,
"Crisis" E-mails, and Junk/SPAM
Strategies

CHAPTER 13

Dealing with Excessive E-mail Carbon Copies, Forwards, and Replies

This may be one of the most practical chapters in the book, because it gets to the heart of where so many people are feeling major pain with their e-mail accounts and e-mail management. This pain comes from dealing with the massive number of messages many of us receive on a regular basis that are in the form of carbon copies, forwarded messages, and replies. What's interesting about these types of e-mails is that many of them are generated simply due to the bad habits of many e-mail senders. I believe that much of this can be explained by the fact that the vast majority of working professionals have never taken a formal training program on effective e-mail management, or that these same professionals have never even just stepped back and thought about their behaviors when it comes to replying to, CC'ing, and forwarding messages. A little bit of common sense can go a long way in terms of solving many of the problems with these types of e-mails. However, we have to take the time to think about what we are doing wrong if we want to make a positive change.

Let's dive in and share some tangible ideas on how to get these types of e-mails under control. We'll start with a new Key Strategy.

KEY STRATEGY #19
End the FYI/"Just Thought You'd Want to Know" E-mails

The e-mail message I most dislike receiving is one that is multiple pages long and has been forwarded from one of my co-workers, clients, or vendors. The person who forwarded the message simply added either "FYI" or "Just thought you'd want to know" to the top of the body text of the message. Why does this message bother me so? For this simple reason: If you forward to me an e-mail that's several pages long and just put "FYI" at the top, you haven't told me what it is about this message that merits my attention. What information contained in the message is important for me to know? Is it the whole message, or just a part of it that is important?

The reason this e-mail irritates me so much is that I have to play "mind reader," and figure out why you deemed the message important enough to forward. Now, I might guess correctly about your intentions, but then again, I might not, and that creates a risk of a miscommunication, an error of omission, and/or several other undesirable consequences. Another reason this type of message bothers me is that it wastes my time! If I'm not sure why the message was forwarded in the first place, I typically have to read the message several times to try to figure out why I received it, and also what I am supposed to do now that I have it. Unless the e-mail you forward is very short and self-explanatory, the "FYI" phrase and its close cousin, "Just thought you'd want to know," are simply way too vague for proper defined action.

So, my strong recommendation is to simply stop sending those vague "FYI" and "Just thought you'd want to know" e-mails.

Let's talk about a different—and much smarter—way to send these e-mails. If you ever forward a message that is longer than a single paragraph (some experts would even say longer than a single sentence), you have to provide the recipient of the message more than simply "FYI" or "Just thought you'd want to know." A better strategy: be quite a bit more specific and list the reasons why you decided to forward this message to the recipient. For example, a message like this is much more usable and specific:

> *Dear Ted,*
> *I'm forwarding this message to you, because, as you'll note on page two of this e-mail, paragraph two, line three, there is a specific deliverable that we need to perform for our client. Can you please confirm that you will complete this deliverable by this date?*
> *Thanks! --Randy [message follows]*

This gives the recipient a lot more information about exactly what needs to be done, and is obviously much better than the vague "FYI" or "Just thought you'd want to know." Sending this kind of message does require a bit more time up front, as the sender must very clearly state what needs to be done, but it saves a large amount of time (and grief!) on the part of the recipient. This is because such a message makes it very easy for the recipient to decipher and determine why that e-mail was forwarded in the first place. Also, by pointing out a specific deliverable and/or due date, the message empowers the recipient to take defined action. This leads to another key strategy.

KEY STRATEGY #20
Consider Only Forwarding or CC'ing Messages in Which All Recipients Have a Defined Task or Action to Complete

As I mentioned earlier, we live in an age of e-mail overload. If we didn't, you probably wouldn't be reading this book right now. A good part of that e-mail overload is made up of forwarded messages and CCs that are either questionable in value or downright unnecessary. A good general rule to help reduce this flow of unnecessary e-mail is to send messages only to people who will have a defined task or action to complete due to the receipt of the e-mail. There's a corollary to this: *Why did you even need to receive the e-mail if you don't have an action to take because of it?* Now, I will be the first to admit that this may not be a perfect rule, and that sometimes there is a benefit in simply sharing information via a forwarded or CC'd e-mail. But I also believe that far too many professionals very casually forward far too many e-mails of questionable informational value simply out of personal convenience, and thus clog up far too many of their colleagues' e-mail inboxes with unnecessary clutter. Do you agree? Can you help fix this problem? Follow this general rule—that every message you forward must contain a deliverable—and a big part of the problem with too many forwards and CCs will go away, especially if you can get your broader team (your co-workers, clients, vendors, and so on) to also follow this same rule.

By the way, if you follow this logic to a T, department-wide forwards and CCs—a major problem in many organizations—should greatly become a thing of the past. This is because every single recipient of the message would need a defined deliverable, and when you send or forward a message to ten or more people, it is not only unlikely that every person will have a defined action, but it may be—from a practical perspective—logistically impossible. Getting your team to adopt this general rule may stop the one or two people in the department who like to copy everybody on everything—which is one of the most common complaints I receive when I lead my "Taming E-mail" seminars.

Now, related to this, here's another sanity strategy that builds right out of the preceding discussion.

KEY STRATEGY #21
Consider Deleting Unnecessary Historical Text When Forwarding or Replying to Messages

If you are about to forward an e-mail that is seven pages long, but the specific deliverable for the recipient is on page two, and all of the information to put the deliverable in proper context is given in pages one through three, is it possible for you to delete the remaining e-mail text from pages four through seven? You might, of course, need to keep some of the message text to keep the message in proper context and give enough information so the recipient can accomplish the defined deliverable appropriately. But, if much of the material after page three is extraneous and unnecessary, why not just delete that text, so the recipient can save some time and also be more focused in terms of what he or she needs to complete? This seems like a pretty straightforward and commonsense strategy that could really save people a lot of time, but it is one that I rarely see people use.

Here's another reason this strategy can be quite helpful: If you delete the unnecessary historical text, you reduce the possibility that "for your eyes only" information (information specifically sent for one—and *only* one—person) will be accidentally forwarded to the wrong person. Have you ever received a forwarded message in which you found a piece of information that maybe you shouldn't have seen? Possibly something that should have remained in confidence between the original senders? I've heard of several examples of this happening—and have even seen one or two of these situations personally—and it almost always has a negative result within or between organizations.

It is obviously very easy in most e-mail programs for people to forward messages or hit "Reply to All." You need to remember this risk whenever you send or forward a message, and mitigate the "accidental forwarding" risk whenever possible by deleting historical text.

A final good reason to delete unnecessary historical text is that very often, that text comes in the form of a string of messages. Often, those messages contain the names and e-mail addresses of past message recipients. If you delete that text, you reduce the risk that those names and/or e-mail addresses will get "pirated" by a junk e-mailer or spammer, and you create a more secure e-mail environment. These people—junk e-mailers and spammers—often are on the lookout for valid e-mail addresses to add to their lists. Deleting the historical text—especially when in the form of "message strings"— helps to protect other e-mailers from receiving more junk and spam.

If we all start deleting unnecessary text, we'll receive the benefit of reduced message load and greater message clarity, which will save all of us a good amount of time and grief.

KEY STRATEGY #22
Change the Subject Line Text When the Subject of the E-mail Changes

Very often people will, in essence, have a conversation via e-mail, meaning that somebody will send an e-mail, and that e-mail will set off a series of replies back and forth between the individuals, which I like to call an e-mail loop. If you are in the midst of one of these e-mail communication loops, and you decide to change the subject of the message (that is, the e-mail is about one topic—one project, one subject, one task—and then, just out of convenience, you hit "Reply" to ask the other party in the loop something on another topic), *please* go up to the top of the e-mail and change the subject line to indicate that you've changed the topic.

You can do this by simply overwriting the subject line. Get rid of all of the "RE: RE: RE: FW:s," and instead, overwrite the existing subject text with the name of the new subject/topic. Because the topic has changed, another smart strategy is to delete all of the previous text from the previous e-mails and previous conversation, for all of the very good reasons mentioned earlier. If you can get yourself into this habit on a regular and consistent basis, you'll greatly reduce the amount of extraneous information (and e-mail addresses) being shared.

KEY STRATEGY #23
Stop the Insanity of Unproductive E-mail Loops

I have witnessed several times in my career what I consider insane e-mail loops, or what I sometimes call "e-mail ping pong". These are e-mail loops that really start to jump back and forth between two or more senders, for a fairly simple and plainly evident reason: someone is having some sort of miscommunication or misunderstanding, and thus the messaging parties keep going back and forth for further clarification. If you ever sense that you've been pulled into one of these insane e-mail loops, you have to consider whether e-mail is even the most efficient and/or effective manner of communication. Very often, a smarter thing to do would be to simply cut off that e-mail loop, pick up the phone, and/or get up from your desk and go find the person. If you can do that—if you can cut off the miscommunication / misunderstanding by having a face-to-face or at least an ear-to-ear conversation—you should be able to save a lot of time and grief for all parties involved. It certainly seems that following this strategy would be a much more effective and efficient use of your time and energy than is trading e-mails back and forth all day long and accomplishing nothing. Investing five minutes in a real conversation—which by the way is always an option (and is something that many professionals seem to have forgotten!)—may save you half an hour or more of aggravating time sending e-mails back and forth.

Now let's take a moment to take a bigger-picture look at these e-mail loops, in which you almost treat your e-mail like instant messaging. Do you remember our earlier discussion about not being a blinger? When you actively participate in these e-mail communication loops, you greatly increase the likelihood that you are going to participate in that bad blinging behavior. And every time you do bling, you create an unneeded interruption for yourself, which, as we discussed earlier, may cause you as much as four to fifteen minutes of lost productivity every time. E-mail loops are close cousins to blinging and usually lead to inefficient behavior that is very damaging to effective productivity. Try to follow a general and simple rule like this: If you want to keep your productivity up, and you sense that you're getting pulled into one of these e-mail communication loops, do yourself a favor and stop the loop. Pick up the phone and call the person, or get up from your desk, go find the person, and have an actual conversation. Another option is this: simply send the person a message asking if you can get together for a five- or ten-minute formally scheduled meeting sometime later that day. Use this meeting time to have an efficient conversation, and to knock out all of the issues that you're currently in discussion about. This certainly makes a lot more sense to me than utilizing your e-mail for instant messaging.

*****

I hope you've enjoyed these strategies on how to gain more sanity with your CCs, forwards, and e-mail communication loops. In the next two chapters, we'll have a deeper discussion about two very specific kinds of forwarded e-mails that can cause major problems for professionals and the companies they work for: CC as a CYA, and an e-mail message I like to call the e-mail "firebomb."

End of Chapter Review Questions:

- What is the problem with lengthy "FYI/Just thought you'd want to know?" e-mails?

- What is a simple solution to help end the overuse of CC'd and forwarded e-mails?

- What are two compelling reasons to delete the unnecessary "historical text" from forwarded messages?

- What is an "unproductive e-mail loop"? What is a simple solution for ending this "e-mail loop?"

Key Strategy Review:

Key Strategy #19: End the FYI/"Just Thought You'd Want to Know" e-mails.

Key Strategy #20: Consider only forwarding or CC'ing messages in which all recipients have a defined task or action to complete.

Key Strategy #21: Consider deleting unnecessary historical text when forwarding or replying to messages.

Key Strategy #22: Change the subject line text when the subject changes.

Key Strategy #23: Stop the insanity of unproductive e-mail loops.

CHAPTER 14

Don't Use CC as a CYA

In the previous chapter, we discussed some commonsense rules for forwarding messages, carbon-copying messages, sending replies, and properly titling the subject of a message. We also discussed deleting historical e-mail text to maintain clarity of purpose, enhance productivity, and protect the owners of the e-mail addresses included in the messages from receiving junk e-mail and spam. In this chapter, I'd like to talk about a particularly nasty little habit of which many professionals are guilty, which is using CC as a CYA. CC, of course, stands for "carbon copy," stemming from the old days of using carbon paper to create typed or written memos in duplicate or triplicate. Of course, we now use CC to add several additional senders to outgoing e-mail messages—a much simpler (and cleaner!) process. In polite terms, CYA stands for "Cover Your Backside," although there is another way that you can phrase this popular aphorism.

When leading my seminars on the topic, I often discuss people frequently using "CC as a CYA." Here are several common "CC as CYA" situations:

- *Upon receiving a new message that contains a task the receiver really doesn't want to do, he sends it to the whole team with the text "Everybody, please notice the task that needs to be done."*

- *A co-worker or client sends a message in which someone is being accusatory or emotional in their language – the receiver then CC's the full team and lets the shouting matches begin.*

- *A message is received that the receiver – for whatever reason – wants everybody in the department or group to see, to establish that it "wasn't her fault." She doesn't care about the fact that it will create hours of distraction and unnecessary discussion in her department – she is covered.*

These, and many more, CC's as CYAs occur every day in corporations and organizations large and small.

Why do the CC senders do this? Basically, to cover their own tracks. After the fact, if something negative happens due to the communication and/or transaction discussed in the e-mail, the person CC'ing everyone on the e-mail will say, "Well, didn't you get the e-mail? This isn't my fault. I sent the e-mail that talked about this exact topic/task/miscommunication/ misunderstanding." In doing so, he or she is attempting to shift the blame from the incident and/or the responsibility for accomplishment of the related task(s) from himself or herself to the multiple recipients of the CC. If the message sent is related to a task that somebody needs to accomplish but is also something that the forwarder doesn't personally want to accomplish, someone in authority might later ask, "Why didn't this task get done?" And the CC'r/forwarder of the e-mail will say, "Well, didn't you get my e-mail? Somebody should have gotten that done. I sent the e-mail." (In essence, this person is saying, "It's not my fault—I passed the buck! Don't look at me for fault here.")

KEY STRATEGY #24
Never CC or forward to a group of people an e-mail that contains an open task with no defined "owner"

Of course, this key strategy is quite similar to Key Strategy #20 from the last chapter: *Consider Only Forwarding or CC'ing Messages Where All Recipients of the Message have a Defined Task or Action to Complete.* But this key strategy is somewhat different in a quite specific way—Key Strategy #20 asks the sender of a message to a large group to make sure *all* recipients have a task and/or deliverable resulting from the message. This is to help reduce the number of unnecessary CC's and forwards. Key Strategy #24 is saying that when there is an open task that someone needs to get done, the e-mail should not be sent until the sender defines and clearly identifies who the specific owner of that task should be.

When I'm leading my e-mail seminars, I remind attendees that just because you sent an e-mail with an open task, it doesn't mean you've bucked your responsibility for the task. If you have not taken the time to define the specific recipients of the message that now have the responsibility for accomplishing the tasks still pending in the message, you as the sender should still ultimately own that responsibility for those tasks (and you should also take the blame if, due to your lack of due diligence, those tasks do not get accomplished properly!) By simply forwarding or carbon copying a message with an open task to a bunch of people without defining ownership/responsibility, you are creating "diffused responsibility" for that task. What this means is that you've spread the responsibility for a single task or multiple tasks across several different individuals, without any of them really knowing who specifically owns the responsibility for accomplishing each and every one of those tasks. In my experience, it is inevitable that one or more of those tasks will not get done, due to the unclear assignment of responsibility.

KEY STRATEGY #25
Remember that diffused responsibility for an e-mail–related task really means NO responsibility.

It is my practical experience that, unless one or more of the receivers of the message step up and overtly assume the responsibility for the embedded task(s), diffused responsibility across several individuals is akin to creating a situation with no responsibility at all. Usually, only bad things can happen when responsibility is diffused across a group without a single "point person" having ultimate ownership of task accomplishment.

In addition, when somebody CC's an entire group of people, that person is bombarding the entire team with a whole bunch more e-mails. Typically, what I've seen is that the people who tend to use CC as a CYA tend to also use it this way quite often. Several times a week, they send out these CC messages, carbon-copying everyone on their team. This can of course significantly add to the sheer volume of messages received by all professionals in the office/team/group. And, of course, if multiple people are sending multiple e-mails to multiple recipients, all with embedded tasks with undefined owners, many important tasks will simply not get done, and the ensuing blame game will begin! (Of course, if companies started holding senders ultimately accountable for e-mail tasks not completed, rather than the receivers, this behavior would likely end very quickly!)

When pressed, many people who use CC as a CYA report

that they are doing this simply because they are trying to keep everyone informed (although the real reason is more likely an effort to shirk responsibility.) The problem with this, as we discussed in the last chapter, is that in this day and age, when people are continuously bombarded with way too many e-mails, this effort to keep everyone "fully informed" is likely to be overkill. Also, it contributes to people having to work extra hours every day, every week, every month, and every year, just trying to keep up with all the CCs and forwards that their teammates are generating and sending.

As I said earlier, I strongly believe that a smart rule for e-mail—a smart but not perfect rule—is to follow the philosophy that if the person receiving an e-mail message does not have a defined task or responsibility with a defined due date coming out of that e-mail, then the recipient most likely didn't need to receive the e-mail in the first place. Following this philosophy may also save you time as a sender of these messages—you will now have many fewer messages to send, and even fewer people to send them to! *(Please reread this paragraph again if this didn't quite sink in – this is a critical e-mail sanity philosophy!)*

The smartest option is to forward a message that contains one or two defined tasks to only the one or two other people that will own and ultimately need to accomplish the actual tasks or activities contained within the e-mail. That could greatly reduce the number of e-mails that you are sending and/or receiving on a regular daily basis, and make work assignments much more clear and unambiguous. And, if you get your whole team following this philosophy, the amount of message clutter generated by your team will drop, while productivity will simultaneously increase, as task assignments become much more clear and accountable. This will all thus positively affect the performance of the whole team/

department/company.

KEY STRATEGY #26
Identify those using "CC as a CYA" and encourage them (mandate for them?) to follow a more sensible e-mail CC/forwarding philosophy.

Related to this Key Strategy, if you find that there is a member of your team who is consistently using CC to either send numerous FYI messages, or is sending messages from a CYA perspective, don't look at this as a serious individual performance problem. This person probably doesn't know any better, and has learned by osmosis from all of the other professionals on the planet who have exhibited similar behavior. Instead, look at this as a training opportunity, especially if you are in the person's supervisory chain. If you see that you have a staff member exhibiting this negative e-mail behavior, look at this as an opportunity to spend five minutes to better train your employee and get him or her to use a much saner and more rational e-mail philosophy, for the benefit of your entire team.

When you receive one of these CCs as a CYA or CCs as an FYI, walk out to the person and say, "Hey, I just received your e-mail and wanted to touch base with you about it. Can you tell me exactly why it is that you sent this message to me and also to the rest of the team?" And let the person answer – let him or her give you the rationale as to why it seemed important to carbon copy everybody. Sometimes, you'll hear a very good reason for e-mailing a message to a larger group – if you hear that, make sure the sender actually includes that rationale at the beginning of the message, rather than just sending messages with the words, "Just thought you'd want to know ...", or, even worse, those three little letters: "FYI." When you do not provide enough text to your team, and only give them "FYI", you leave the team guessing as to what is the importance and value of the message, or what needs to be done. People aren't mind readers – if you send a message with important information, make the important information painfully clear!

Now, very often, when you ask the sender why they sent the message, you'll instead hear back something like this, "Well, I just thought everybody would want to know," or "I felt it was important to share this information across the entire team," without any real specifics, or even, "Well, I really didn't know what to do with this information, or if it was even important, so I just forwarded it on to everyone else." When you hear something like that, say, "Yeah, I understand. But you have to remember we're all getting way too many e-mails these days—so many that it is hard for us to keep up. And if everybody on the team follows the philosophy you just mentioned, we're going to spend all day every day just doing our e-mail and never getting any work done. Of course, that is not a tenable option. We need to find a better way to do this."

Then say to him or her, "Here's what I propose: If you are going to send out an e-mail to the rest of the team, I'd like to see a written rationale at the start of the message as to why it was sent to the rest of the team, and I would also like each and every recipient of the e-mail to have a message-related task that they need to accomplish. If they don't have a defined deliverable, then don't include them in the message. We've all got plenty of work to do—it is functionally impossible for all of us to know all the time what everyone else is working on. If top management deems that everyone needs a status update, top management will call a meeting or send out an update memo. But we just can't have everyone doing this all of the time."

If possible, also request that the sender add in whatever necessary specifics will make the message more usable (for example, who owns each task, what the due dates are, how the team will report back on success and/or problems, and so on). In essence, you are just asking him or her to slow down a bit, and take the time to think about who really needs and doesn't need to receive a message and why it is they need to receive it, as well as taking the time to clearly define responsibilities for the recipients. Just by getting the sender to take a little extra time to think about what they are sending before they send it, you will save a great amount of time for those receiving the messages. And once you inform the sender that people in the department are receiving too many e-mails, he or she may not feel such a strong need to be constantly CC'ing people and may get more disciplined about sending messages—not sending nearly as many, nearly as often, thus greatly reducing the flow of e-mail coming from any particular party. Of course, if this is a problem for many people on your team, it might even be a good opportunity for a little staff discussion.

By getting your team to follow these new philosophies, ownership of tasks and responsibilities will be clearer, e-mail clutter will drop, staff will feel more appropriately empowered, and productivity will increase. And people might not dread opening their e-mail as much—just one more way to tame that e-mail beast!

Now, let's discuss one final very devious type of sent or forwarded message—the e-mail "firebomb."

End of Chapter Review Questions:

• Why is it that so many people use e-mail "CC as a CYA"?

- What is "diffused responsibility" when related to e-mails and the tasks embedded within them?

- Who should ultimately own the responsibility for a task that doesn't get completed due to "diffused responsibility"?

- When someone on your team sends out too many "CC/FYI" messages, what can you do to help your team regain e-mail sanity?

Key Strategy Review:

Key Strategy #24: Never CC or forward to a group of people an e-mail that contains an open task with no defined "owner".

Key Strategy #25: Remember that diffused responsibility for an e-mail–related task really means *no* responsibility.

Key Strategy #26: Identify those using "CC as a CYA" and encourage them (mandate for them?) to follow a more sensible e-mail CC/forwarding philosophy.

CHAPTER 15

How to Handle the E-mail "Firebomb"

Now, let's discuss a particularly devious kind of e-mail—one that can cause major problems and damage not only to individuals, but also to the broader companies that they work for. This e-mail is what I like to call the "firebomb." The best way I can describe an e-mail firebomb is this—the moment that it comes into your inbox, the e-mail feels like it is ticking, loaded with content that could be explosive. When I say "explosive," I mean that it is an e-mail that is delivering information regarding an impending or current crisis for your organization. If not dealt with properly, it may cause panic and/or major distress in your organization.

Let me share a fun little example from my seminars: Let's say that you work for a privately held company. The president of the company is the owner, and the president's son works for the company. At the company's summer picnic, the president's son makes inappropriate advances on your primary client's daughter. This primary client is worth millions of dollars a year in business. The client, in a rage, sends an e-mail to you, his key contact in the company, about how he is just about to end this very lucrative relationship with your organization. You know that if he does this, it may cause serious financial distress for your organization, possibly even bankruptcy.

This e-mail would most definitely be an "e-mail firebomb." By the way, you can also receive similar firebombs by phone, fax, certified letter—even in person. But, because it is so easy to immediately send and forward e-mails to a number of people, e-mail firebombs potentially may be both more common and more explosive than the firebombs delivered in other forms of communication.

Often I've seen situations in which people receive an e-mail firebomb like the example I described, and they respond in the worst way possible—they panic! They read the e-mail and, in a panic, send it out to a broad distribution list with a title like, "URGENT CRISIS—EVERYONE READ IMMEDIATELY!" If they bother to put any kind of a cover note at all on the message, it is typically rife with panic—"This is potentially a disaster. What do we do? Help!" Of course, what follows after that is the ensuing and now unavoidable disaster. (This is much like spreading gasoline on a fire!) Everyone who receives the message starts to take "panicked" action, most likely in a highly uncoordinated manner, which may cause more harm than good—especially, in this case, if the company president's son is one of the people on the e-mail distribution list. He may try to jump in and make a phone call to either the daughter or the client to "make things right," and, of course, all he's going to do is make things worse!

At this point I like to remind readers of a very popular book from the 1970s by Douglas Adams, a British science fiction humorist. The book is called *The Hitchhiker's Guide to the Galaxy*—a sci-fi comedy classic. In this book, Adams envisioned a device that was basically a super-powered PDA.

(How about that? He envisioned that all the way back in the '70s!) What was truly interesting was that this "Hitchhikers Guide to the Galaxy" had a little leather cover, which was embossed with just two words: "Don't Panic." Not only is this an appropriate strategy for those embarking on a hitchhiking tour through our galaxy, I believe it is also an appropriate starter strategy for handling e-mail firebombs, and just about everything else that you'll face in your life. "Don't panic"—an excellent mantra!

KEY STRATEGY #27
When You Receive an E-mail Firebomb, Don't Panic!

Here's what I suggest you do if you receive a message that seems to be an e-mail firebomb:

1. First thing: Don't panic. Take a deep breath.

2. Second thing: Determine whether or not you are the owner of the bomb (in other words, the person who will lead the "bomb squad" that will attempt to "defuse" the bomb).

3. If you are the person in your organization who will "lead the bomb squad", the appropriate thing for you to do is take a moment to look over the message, and, before you even mention its receipt and existence to another person, develop some form of a working plan to defuse this bomb.

4. Once you have a plan for handling this firebomb, you need to do one of two things:

   a. Send out a message with very specific instructions to a few key people you can trust. In this message, explain why this e-mail is a firebomb—what the situation is that is causing the crisis—and also what the recipients' specific steps are in terms of following actions they need to take to help you with diffusing the situation and defusing the bomb. Or . . .

b. The second option—one that I prefer even more—is this: rather than sending an e-mail with those instructions, print out several copies of the e-mail and call each of the people on your newly defined "bomb squad" into an emergency meeting or teleconference with the goal of sharing what's in the e-mail, as well as your best-effort assessment of an appropriate action plan. Then, spend the rest of the meeting getting everyone on the same page so they can take coordinated appropriate action to help defuse the bomb.

5. Once you follow steps A or B above, begin to execute your coordinated bomb-defusing plan.

Of course, just following these steps does not guarantee that you will not trigger the bomb. But if you do follow these steps, you will at least greatly increase your odds of defusing the bomb—of effectively solving the crisis situation.

Remember this—in a situation where there is a lot of emotion, a lot of potential misinterpretation, and a lot of possibility for error, e-mail is sometimes not at all the right medium to use for communication. In those situations, conversation may be best! An emergency meeting is an option, and it is one that effective managers should never forget as a viable and necessary management tool in times of crisis. (We'll talk more about appropriate communication options other than e-mail in the next chapter.)

Now let's assume that, after following the "don't panic" rule, you make a determination that this is a firebomb that you don't really own. (Of course, if it is in your inbox alone, you do own it until you find someone else willing to take it!) Following is what I recommend you do after you determine that the appropriate person to own the message—to defuse the bomb and diffuse the situation—is another person in your group or team.

First, forward the e-mail directly to the person you believe truly owns it, and at the top of the message, write either "I'll be calling right now", or "I'll be right over." Then, send the message and make the call or go find that person!

Do everything within your power to find that person and explain what you've just put into his or her e-mail box. Or, if the person is handy and nearby, simply print the message and walk it over—call a quick little impromptu "emergency conversation" type of meeting with that person. Say, "Look at this message. It looks like it is fraught with danger—a possible crisis. I believe that you are the right person for this, and that you need to own it. I want to confirm with you that you agree, and that you are going to take appropriate actions to move forward. It is now your bomb to defuse." Of course, before you can walk away from that e-mail firebomb, you need to get the person's agreement that he or she now owns the bomb. That person might turn right back around to you to ask for your help in defusing the bomb, but at least he or she is now the point person. Finally, recommend that this person follow the steps outlined in the previous section for defusing the bomb!

KEY STRATEGY #28

Before handing off any important e-mail, including those carrying a potential crisis, verify that the person being handed the e-mail accepts and agrees to take ownership and re-

sponsibility for the e-mail and any embedded tasks/deliverables.

In both of these circumstances, you followed the critical "don't panic" rule. You at least didn't pour gasoline on the fire and make the crisis worse. You either identified the appropriate owner or took ownership and built an appropriate response plan. Either way, you at least decreased the likelihood that the bomb is going to go off, or will at least not be as damaging as it might have been. Sure, there are no guarantees in either of these circumstances, but at least you've greatly helped your team by giving them a chance to manage the situation and the crisis more appropriately. In addition, by keeping your cool and following a plan in a time of crisis and challenge, you've shown you have what it takes to be an effective and regarded leader in your organization.

Speaking of being an effective leader, let's now talk about a communications tool that many professionals seem to have forgotten about due to the ease of e-mail, yet still should be first and foremost in the tool kit of any truly effective leader and manager: a live conversation!

End of Chapter Review Questions:

- What is an "e-mail firebomb"?

- What is the first thing you need to keep yourself from doing when you receive an e-mail firebomb?

- When handing off an e-mail firebomb to someone else, what is the first critical thing you need to verify with that person?

- What is one communications option to never forget when faced with an e-mail firebomb, or any other critical communications/workplace/interpersonal challenge or crisis?

Key Strategy Review:

Key Strategy #27: When you receive an e-mail firebomb, *don't panic!*

Key Strategy #28: Before handing off any important e-mail, including those carrying a potential crisis, verify that the person being handed the e-mail accepts and agrees to take ownership and responsibility for the e-mail and any embedded tasks/deliverables.

CHAPTER 16

E-mail and the Lost Art of Conversation

One thing in particular is pretty amazing to me when I look back over the fifteen to twenty years that most of us have had exposure to a personal or professional e-mail account. It seems that in that time, many of us have lost the ability to hold an effective, professional conversation. E-mail has become our "crutch," and we've learned to let e-mail do much of our dirty work for us. We've learned to use e-mail as our surrogate for having a live personal conversation.

In a lot of circumstances, that actually does make sense. If the communication is quick, if the task is clear, if the outcome desired is obvious, e-mail is a great tool. It speeds up the communication and allows the person receiving the message to deal with it at the appropriate time, in many cases without having to refer back to the sender, assuming that the e-mail has all of the information that the recipient needs.

But not every communication and not every circumstance is quite that simple. As a matter of fact, they often are much more complicated than that. In the previous chapter, we talked about the e-mail firebomb. Earlier, we talked about e-mail communication loops in which it is obvious that there is an ongoing misunderstanding or miscommunication between two or more parties. Yet even in those situations, people still insist on using e-mail because they perceive it to be "easy." The problem is, of course, that e-mail is not really the easy solution. It is instead a highly inefficient communications solution in these circumstances. You are likely to spend a whole lot of time going back and forth trying to get people to understand something or to properly handle something that they are not likely to understand well or handle well. You will probably have to spend significant extra time in these situations because the e-mail messages will cause unintended, inappropriate circumstances or outcomes, thus causing potential crises and chaos in your organization, or at the bare minimum, significant rework on your part as well as on the part of others.

KEY STRATEGY #29

In Every Communications Situation, Consider Whether or Not E-mail Is the Most Efficient and/or Effective Communication Method.

Whether you're dealing with an e-mail firebomb, an e-mail communication loop, or any one of a number of other e-mail situations, the better option may be simply finding the person or people involved in the matter, and then having a real conversation by telephone, or even an impromptu in-person meeting, rather then sending a stream of e-mails with to-be-expected negative consequences. As I do my consultations with many businesses, corporations, and organizations, I always try to remind my clients that conversation and impromptu meetings may be the most effective and efficient form of communication you can consider and use in any given interpersonal communications situation, from both a personnel management and morale perspective, as well as from a cost-benefit perspective, due to the decreased risk of misunderstandings, mistakes, errors of omission, and rework. I strongly recommend that just about every professional and every manager consider redeploying live conversation and impromptu meetings as part of their management and productivity arsenal. You can use these tools; you can use them well; and you can see a productivity, profitability, and staff development/morale benefit from doing these things. Remember, e-mail is easy, but if the subject or content of the e-mail is fraught with the possibility of miscommunication, misinterpretation, or misunderstanding; if it is loaded with emotional content; or if it is potentially explosive—e-mail is most likely the wrong form of communication to use. You need to consider whether other communication options will give you the best opportunity to meet the productivity and professional goals of a given situation.

Sometimes, as already mentioned, a live one-on-one in-person or telephone conversation, or even an impromptu meeting, may be a better option for getting everyone fully understanding each other, reaching consensus, and creating an appropriate and smart plan for follow-up action. Remember also that there are other technology-enhanced communication tools outside of e-mail that may allow you to better facilitate effective interpersonal communications. Never forget the option of a three-way call, a teleconference call, a videoconference, a Web-enhanced conference call (conference call via a Web-based VoIP service), a teleseminar (a training or speaking program delivered via a teleconference call service), or a webinar (a training or speaking program delivered via Web-based VoIP service with live sharing of multiple computer desktops to share presentations, software demonstrations, and so on). Yes, you have many more options than just sending an e-mail to more effectively communicate with your team!

KEY STRATEGY #30

Never forget about the other technology-enabled communications tools that might be better options for a given interpersonal communications situation.

All of these options are reasonably cost-effective, especially when compared to the travel and time cost usually experienced when getting geographically dispersed parties together in person, and they potentially give you the opportunity to facilitate a more open and effective conversation and/or meeting when either or both is the right thing to do. Keep these tools in mind when you take a look at which options best meet your business circumstance or situation. If you have never used these technology-enhanced tools, it is probably time that you learned about their costs and capabilities, as well as how to begin utilizing them. They are important additions to any competent manager's or leader's tool kit.

One final suggestion regarding the lost art of conversation: don't police just yourself on this, especially if you have staff management responsibilities. Keep your eyes open to see if other members of your staff are utilizing e-mail inappropriately for certain kinds of communications, especially in situations where a conversation, meeting, or technology-enhanced communications tool would make a lot more sense. If you happen to be copied on a CYA or FYI message, or if you happen to see people blasting e-mails back and forth in one of those wasteful e-mail communications loops—especially if you see they are making little side comments about how the loop is not a good use of their time—take a moment and to inject some sanity and common sense back into the situation. Say to them, "Hey, how about just walking over and talking to the person? Or maybe you could just pick up the phone. Have you considered setting up a three-way call? Maybe these are better ways to handle this discussion so you folks don't keep going around and around in circles." Utilize these circumstances as training opportunities. Get the staff members who report to you to also identify when e-mail is not the most effective form of communication, and to identify when another communication tool may be more efficient, effective, and appropriate. And get them trained on how to actually use these tools. Most of the time, the reason they don't use these other tools is that they don't know how. If this is the case, help them learn how!

I'm always surprised by how many managers and professionals have no idea how to make a three-way call, set up a teleconference, or hold a webinar. I'm even more surprised when they don't know who to call to help them do these things. There are almost always internal or external consultants who can set up these things for just about any professional firm or organization. Having these tools within easy reach should be a "given" for any functional professional, manager, or leader. Utilizing these tools, when and if appropriate, can only help you personally—and your firm more broadly—to achieve your stated goals and aspirations. Get these tools in reach, and start using them.

On a related note, if you find that your staff has actually lost the ability to hold real business conversations in a professional and courteous manner – with planned agendas, action items, and follow-up deliverables – hire a trainer or consultant to come in and deliver a program on these topics for your organization. There are many top-notch experts in these areas—find one that fits the style of your firm, and get them in-house until your staff has the ability to start effectively talking with each other again. You'll never find a better investment of your time and/or money. As I've said previously, much of this is common sense; you just probably haven't thought of it this way. Now is the time to start thinking about these things, and using these tools for more effective and productive behavior and results. And never forget option #1: a live, real conversation between two or more adults!

A Quick Tip: *Use Your E-mail to Make Your Phone Calls Go Better.* I have to give a quick thanks to Duane Johnson in California for providing this excellent quick tip: if you ever have a planned phone call with another party scheduled, consider sending a brief e-mail to that party with 2-4 agenda items on what is to be covered during the call. In essence, you are creating a formal "meeting" agenda for your phone call, which will allow all parties on the call to be better prepared, make the phone call shorter and more efficient, and allow for a better distribution of work after the call. Great tip Duane!

End of Chapter Review Questions:

• When is e-mail often the worst form of communications tool to use in a given interpersonal communications situation?

• What are two other highly preferred communications options to remember when dealing with confusing, emotional, or complex communications situations?

• What are some other technology-enabled communications options to remember when facing these interpersonal communications situations?

Key Strategy Review:

Key Strategy #29: In every communications situation, consider whether or not e-mail is the most efficient and/or effective communication method.

Key Strategy #30: Never forget about the other technology-enabled communications tools that might be better options for a given interpersonal communications situation.

Chapter 17

Junk and Spam Strategies

I believe this chapter is going to surprise you, simply because it may seem fairly short, especially considering how much of a problem spam has been reported to be by many people. Part of the reason that this is going to be a short chapter is that I believe if you've already followed some of the strategies shared earlier – including the strategy of having a defined Internet account for all of your e-commerce related activities – you've already taken a big step toward protecting your primary work and personal e-mail accounts from being identified by and inundated by spammers. Also don't forget the strategy of deleting legacy copy from the e-mails you are sending, so that it is less easy for spammers to get access to you and your co-workers' e-mail addresses.

By doing this, you should be able to greatly reduce the amount of spam that you have in your inbox. Added to all of this is the fact that many organizations and corporations already have a quite robust spam filter (by the way, I highly encourage you to speak with your IT staff and learn how to use the filter most effectively). All of these strategies should help ensure that spam will become a somewhat minimal issue in your life and in your e-mail adventures.

That being said, spam is still something that needs to be

dealt with, and I say needs to be dealt with ruthlessly. Right now, you are probably wondering, "Why does spam even exist?" I did a little research on this topic a couple of years ago, and read an article that indicated that a spammer who is actually selling a legitimate product or service only needs about one person out of 40,000 to respond to the message in order to make a profit from it—one out of 40,000! Now compare that to the direct mail industry (of interest, I spent several years doing direct response and direct mail marketing early in my career), where you need a ½ to 1 percent response to make money, and you can see why spam has become so ubiquitous. In traditional direct mail activities, one out of 100 to one out of 200 is what you need to make a profit; with e-mail spam, all you need is one out of 40,000!

What is even more interesting is that many of the spammers out there these days are not trying to run legitimate for-profit enterprises. They are instead up to no good, with many of them related to organized crime. Add to that the fact that many of the most sophisticated spam operations are offshore now—often in unregulated third-world countries with significantly less stringent rules and laws preventing spam—and that means there really isn't a heck of a lot you can do about spam, at least to stop it. (In the United States, spam is regulated and policed by the Federal Trade Commission [FTC]. It is the responsibility of that agency to find and prosecute illegal spam operations. However, many offshore operations are outside the jurisdiction of the FTC. The only way the FTC can crack down on these rogue operators is through sophisticated multi-country investigations and prosecutions—which is by all measures a relatively low priority with everything else going on globally these days.)

Spam is here, it is going to stay, and there's nothing in the upcoming future that would indicate that it's going to be going away any time soon. There are just too many people out there likely to fall for these things to keep it from going away. Unfortunately, much of spam these days is purely fraudulent in nature. Not only are spammers trying to sell products that are fully misrepresented (for example, pharmaceutical products or software programs for one-tenth of the actual market price that are anything but the real thing, if you receive anything at all), many spammers are actually trying to gather your financial and personal information, and utilize that information to commit fraud against you (identity theft, bank account access, credit card fraud, and so on).

To do this, many spammers engage in an activity called "phishing." What they do is send out official-looking communications via e-mail that often seems legitimate and connected to a well-known corporation (for example, your bank, credit union, mortgage operation, investment firm, or something like that). They are so good at this and so sophisticated now, they can fool almost any untrained person, and the messages are so well put together that they do indeed seem to be a valid communication from an organization that you have done business with before.

KEY STRATEGY #31
Become Ruthless at Identifying and Deleting Possible Spam.

You've got to get good at quickly identifying spam, and then taking ruthless action with it. If you can quickly identify and delete received spam, or report it to your spam filter, you will save countless minutes every day that can be better used on value-producing activities. I did a little research recently, and found that one of the leading online payment vendors, PayPal, recently published a list of nine key spam/

spoof identifiers, which I am going to share here (I will add some editorial comments following each of the identifiers, in parentheses):

9 Ways to Recognize Spam E-mails—*List from PayPal, editorial from Randy Dean (in parentheses)* + **One Bonus Identifier by Randy Dean**

1. **Generic Greetings.** (Be very wary of the "Hi, How Have You Been" e-mails you receive from people you are not familiar with—this is likely spam.)

2. **A Fake Sender's Address.** (If the name on the e-mail doesn't match the e-mail address [i.e. From: Sarah Stevens (bobsmith@abccorp.com)], don't trust it!)

3. **A False Sense of Urgency.** (If you don't know the sender, and especially if it is asking for personal or financial information ASAP, don't fall for the urgency.)

4. **Fake Links.** (A spammer that is using an HTML-formatted e-mail can make a link that looks like it is going to a legitimate Web site/Web page, but is actually going to a bogus site or page, likely with ill intent. When in doubt, hand-type the URL address into your browser rather than clicking on the link.)

5. **E-mails that Appear to Be Websites.** (If an e-mail looks like a Web page, and offers active links or data entry boxes, be very wary. I'd recommend *never* entering data into an entry box on a received e-mail—at bare minimum, it is an "unsecured" data transfer, and in the worst case, you are likely about to become a victim of phishing.)

6. **Misspellings and Bad Grammar.** (It is obvious that many spammers were not English majors in college—look for misspellings, bad grammar, and so on. Most professional communications sent by legitimate firms are carefully

reviewed by a professional proofreader, and thus, errors in spelling and grammar are unlikely.)

7. **Unsafe Sites.** (If you are forwarded to a Web site asking for your personal or financial data, that site should require a login to an "https" page [secure data transmission page] before asking for that proprietary information. If you are not on an "https" page, be careful before submitting data.)

8. **Pop-up Boxes.** (Be careful clicking on or submitting information via a pop-up box. They are almost always not secure. Be wary of any e-mailer embedding a pop-up within an e-mail communication.)

9. **Dangerous Attachments.** (If you do not inherently trust the sender of a message that has an attachment [or, in some cases, the original sender of the attachment], be very leery of opening the attachment—especially if it is a file type that you are not familiar with. You could be inadvertently downloading spyware or adware, or possibly launching a virus. See the next section for more about this.)

I will add one more item to this list:

10. **"Photo" spam.** Do not trust any message in which the body copy and all graphics are created not with actual text, but instead are a digital photograph of a document (often a JPEG or BMP file). Many spammers are now using "photo" spam because photographed documents do not trigger spam filters as often as do e-mails containing written text. Some even put real text that is designed to get around a spam filter in the background behind the photographed document; all the recipient sees is the photographed document, but all that a spam filter sees is the background text.

These are the things to watch for to help you identify not only spam, but also the phishing types of e-mails and communications. Following these strategies will also help you to avoid downloading spyware, adware, or a virus. For your information, spyware is a small executable program that allows an outside user to "watch" your activities while you are connected to the Web, while adware feeds information back to certain data collection companies—some with less-than-honest intentions—so that marketers can create Internet-based offers for you and track your Web surfing preferences. These programs can be particularly devious, not only from an information security perspective, but also because they can interfere with the normal running of your computer because they run in the background and eat up your available RAM, thus making your computer run slower and possibly locking up your computer when too many programs are running.

This leads to a couple of spam strategies that I'd like to share and discuss a bit more deeply.

KEY STRATEGY #32
Never open a suspicious e-mail attachment.

If a message seems suspicious, never open its attachment. If you believe that an e-mail might be spam, do not open any files or executables attached to that e-mail. Not only could you open a file with an executable spyware or adware program embedded, you might open a file significantly more devious— perhaps a full-blown, take-over-your-hard-drive virus. Save yourself the worry by following a simple philosophy: *"When in doubt, toss it out!"*

Related to this, here is a GREAT key strategy for dealing with junk and spam e-mails when using PC-based commercial e-mail programs, like MS Outlook, Lotus Notes, or GroupWise:

KEY STRATEGY #33
Use the "Shift-Delete" keystroke combination to bypass your "Deleted Items" folder and knock likely junk/spam e-mails completely out of your account.

Here's how you use the "Shift-Delete" keystroke combination on a likely junk/spam e-mail message: First, single left-click the suspected message to select it (don't double-click the message – that will open it and may make your account/computer vulnerable.) Then, hold down the "Shift" key and then hit the "Delete" key with the "Shift" key still depressed. That's it! Your message is now gone – it isn't in your inbox any longer, it isn't in your deleted items folder – it is gone! (In Microsoft Outlook, you'll even get a "dummy message" asking you "Are you sure you want to delete this message?" Just click "Enter" when you get this message, and now the message is gone!) Now, if you do just hit the single "Delete," make sure to follow through and once again delete all messages from your "Deleted Items" folder if you have any suspected junk or spam messages in that folder.

KEY STRATEGY #34
Don't click on an embedded URL or web address/hyperlink unless you implicitly trust the sender of the message.

As mentioned in the PayPal list of identifiers, another thing to be very wary of is a URL (active Web link) embedded within an e-mail, especially if you do not fully trust the sender of a forwarded message (or, in some cases, the original sender of the e-mail.)

When at all in doubt about a message and an affiliated embedded URL, consider doing the following things to help protect yourself: 1) Call the person who sent the e-mail (if you know him or her personally), and ask if the e-mail and the related links are legitimate. If that person says anything less than "Absolutely," don't click on the links! I'm sure that many "I think so's" were followed by major computer viruses, identity thefts, or security breaches. 2) If you don't know the sender, you should retype the given URL directly into your Web browser by hand; go to the primary Web site listed, instead of a specific URL; possibly even call the company that the e-mail claims to be representing to verify the message and links are valid (especially if that company is one of your primary financial institutions—most financial institutions *never* will ask for you to submit needed information via e-mail); or, just delete the message.

KEY STRATEGY #35
Never enter information into an open box or field in a received e-mail.

Finally, never, ever, ever enter information into an open box or field in an e-mail message! If an e-mail gives you a simple "reply box" with a submit button, asking you to enter your e-mail address, your name, your phone number, your home or work address, or your account number, or any other identifying personal information, you are most likely about to be phished. Almost always, these kinds of queries will be directed to an illegitimate, phishing organization. These people are sophisticated. If they gather a little bit of information from you in the first e-mail, that might not be enough to get you, but once they get a little piece of needed information, they will keep after you with a concerted effort, utilizing e-mails (and possibly also snail mail and telephone inquiries), often referring to different URLs, Web sites, phone numbers, and even bogus corporations to gather one piece of data at a time, until they get all the information they need to go in and wipe away your bank account. That's their plan—they're trying to steal your money. And they're going to do whatever they can to try to gather those little pieces of information until they have enough to get you.

"Spoofing"

Most often, today's spammers are rotating the e-mail addresses they are using to send spam, meaning that they will not use the same e-mail address more than once or twice to send a spam message. They know that many organizations have spam filters, and that people can report spam to the filter, thus "blacklisting" future messages from that sender. To avoid getting blacklisted and to keep getting their messages through, spammers actively steal legitimate e-mail addresses from legitimate companies—an action called "spoofing." They find a legitimate e-mail address, use a fairly simple process to briefly "hijack" that address, send a big batch of spam through that address for a day or two, and then drop that address and find another one, to start the process over again.

Because of this, reporting a spam message to your company's spam filter the first time it happens may actually be doing a disservice to your organization. You might be telling your spam filter that a legitimate sender/organization is a spammer when the message sender actually has been spoofed. Except for this one batch of e-mails that was sent by the external spammer, everything else from this sender is true and legitimate. But now, your corporate spam filter will no longer let any of the sender's legitimate messages get through—not only to you, but often to all of the other people in your organization. I feel some personal pain with this— my company's domain has been targeted by spoofers about three times in the past two years. I know because I receive the "Undeliverable Message" reports in my live account when it happens, and I can often see the spam message that was sent not by me, but by a spammer using my company's domain name. What is really aggravating is that, because most of these jokers are located overseas, there is really very little I can do to stop them. Because of this, I recommend the next Key Strategy.

KEY STRATEGY #36
"Blacklist" only identified <u>repeat</u> spammers

If you receive spam messages that seem to be consistently coming from the same e-mail address and/or sender—spam from the same sender more than once or twice—that is a good time to consider using the "reporting spam" options provided in your e-mail software or by your organization. In Microsoft Outlook you can simply right-click and report an e-mail as either junk or spam—this is an available "right click" option every time you have a message selected. Learn how to use this function.

Also, if you are provided with an organizational spam filter from your company's IT group, learn how to properly use it. If you report repeat spammers to your companywide filter, you'll be able to also keep your co-workers from getting these annoying and sometimes damaging messages. Finally, if you believe that the person spamming you is located in the United States, you can forward that e-mail to the FTC by utilizing the following address: *spam@FTC.gov*. Forward a copy of the e-mail address and the message to this address. The FTC may be able to identify the person responsible for the spam and stop him or her from doing this further. There recently was a major conviction of a U.S.-based spammer who was sending several million spam messages every week. He was living a millionaire's lifestyle in a mansion on a private island in Puget Sound—all from proceeds netted from spam. There are only two ways to stop these people: 1) stop buying products or services from them; 2) report them and help them get caught, when and if possible.

Internet-based e-mail vendors such as Yahoo!, Hotmail, and Gmail typically have a spam-reporting capability. You can report any likely spam message (or even those more dastardly phishing types of e-mails) to your service. If the spam was sent by one of its users, the vendor might actually shut down that user for breaking its "terms of service" agreement (sending spam is typically forbidden by Internet e-mail vendors.) That might at least slow them down on bugging you again!

One caveat: Although I always encourage you to report repeat spammers, either to your spam filter/IT staff, the FTC, or your Internet-based e-mail provider, you have to always think about whether this is a worthwhile use of your time. As I said earlier, the vast majority of spam messages these days come from overseas organizations that are often linked to organized crime. The FTC can't really stop them. These spammers also are likely to be spoofing legitimate addresses and thus rotating the addresses they use to send their spam, making it difficult to really get them. It may not be worth your effort from a "time spent" perspective; even if you report them, you are probably not going to stop them—you are still going to get messages from the spammer. If that is the case, it might just be smarter and easier to use the "Shift-Delete" strategy we mentioned earlier in the chapter, and keep moving forward with your work. You will have to make that call.

Spam E-mail versus Junk E-mail

Now I'd like to talk about one other type of nuisance e-mail that isn't really spam in my mind—instead, I call it "junk." Junk e-mail is basically like the junk mail that you receive in your mailbox at home. It usually does have a legitimate business purpose, and the person sending it is usually trying to sell a legitimate product or service, or at least is trying to provide information that is true and useful. However, because of your personal preferences, needs, and desires, you determine that you don't really want to or need to be getting those messages. For you, it is junk, but for the sender and for many of the people receiving the messages, the messages are actually valuable.

KEY STRATEGY #37
Unsubscribe or auto-delete junk e-mails versus reporting as spam.

When you are dealing with junk e-mail instead of spam, I do recommend a slightly different mentality and philosophy. Here is that philosophy: very often, when you are added to an e-mail list or decide to subscribe to a subscription-based e-mail newsletter or list that you later determine is "junk" for you, remember that what's junk to you may be very valuable to another. Many people, once they no longer see the value of the messages, decide to report these messages as spam. I would ask that you not do that—rather than reporting it as spam, either use the "Unsubscribe" or "Remove from list" options provided by the sender (most legitimate e-mail marketers readily and easily provide these options because they do not want to be "blacklisted"), or, just use the right-click options discussed earlier, and create a rule to automatically delete any messages sent from this sender. Thus, the messages are deleted as soon as they come in and will not bother you or waste your time, but they will also not be labeled as spam. Most professional e-mail marketing programs and services—services like Constant Contact, Aweber, and others—allow for an "opt out" option on every single message that is sent. Utilize this option instead of reporting such messages as spam. If they are legitimate organizations selling legitimate products and services, and they are using e-mail marketing ethically and appropriately, there is absolutely no reason that they shouldn't be allowed to utilize e-mail as an effective and targeted marketing tool.

I personally subscribe to several e-mail newsletters and product/service update lists that I very much like to be a part of. If people in my organization started to report those newsletters and update lists as spam, I would not be able to receive such messages in the future – my spam filter would start knocking them out. So, do your co-workers a favor and learn to use the opt-out/unsubscribe options or set up a rule to auto-delete these messages rather than reporting them as spam. Doing this will not only help greatly reduce the amount of junk e-mail you are receiving, it will also help the economy and information product and service providers (like me!) to grow and prosper.

KEY STRATEGY #38
Consider setting up a rule to auto-file e-newsletters and e-zines in an inbox subfolder.

Do you ever receive messages that at times are somewhat

of a nuisance, but at other times contain information that you actually rather enjoy receiving or that you find useful? Typically, e-newsletters and e-zines that you receive in your e-mail account (and that you have often personally subscribed to) fall into this category. When you aren't too busy, you like to receive this information to keep abreast of what is going on in your field, your industry, or in an area of personal interest or passion. But when you are busy, they start to clog up your e-mail inbox and become a nuisance.

If you have any messages like that, another option you can strongly consider is once again utilizing one of the "rules" options that are available when you select and right-click on a message in Outlook (and possibly other commercial e-mail programs). Instead of setting up a rule that auto-deletes these messages, instead use the option that allows you to auto-file the messages from that sender into a specified folder. For example, let's say that you receive a weekly or monthly e-newsletter from a particular organization. Many times when you receive it, you're just too busy to look at it, but every once in a while, you actually enjoy reading the content.

You can set up a rule so that whenever a message is received from the sender of the e-newsletter, it is automatically filed into a designated folder inside of your inbox. You could create a "Great Ideas Enews" folder in your inbox, and then auto-file your monthly "Great Ideas" e-newsletter messages directly into that folder when received. Without your having to do anything else, those messages will accumulate in this folder until you take the time periodically to read through them or delete them. They are there if you want them, but out of your way if you don't have the time. (You could even set up your auto-archiving and auto-deletion properties in this folder to automatically delete these messages once they get a few months old!) Use this strategy for the "sometimes a nuisance, sometimes not" e-mails, and keep your productivity and business intelligence growing consistently.

This is a good time for another video tip! In this one, I'll show you how to "right-click" to create rules for both auto-deleting messages from a specified sender as well as auto-filing messages from a specified sender.

Video Tutorial #9: *Using the "rules" options to auto-delete and/or auto-file messages from specific senders.*

Remember to visit the Taming E-mail Reader web site at: http://www.tamingemailreader.com/videotutorials.html to see this and all of the other related video tutorials from *Taming the E-mail Beast.*

In closing, here is a "reminders" list of key spam/junk e-mail strategies:

- Get efficient at identifying spam, and ruthless in dealing with it (use Shift-Delete to painlessly get rid of likely spam).

- Use "Shift-Delete" to completely delete junk and spam messages from your commercial e-mail account in one simple step.

- Never open a suspicious e-mail attachment.

- Don't click on an embedded URL unless you implicitly trust the sender of the message.

- Never enter information into an open box or field in a received e-mail.

- Report and/or blacklist identified repeat spammers.

- Unsubscribe from or auto-delete junk e-mails versus reporting them as spam.

- Consider setting up a rule to autofile e-newsletters in a folder in your inbox.

End of Chapter Review Questions:

- Why is spam both so common and so pervasive (think financial!)?

- What are a couple key strategies we've already shared earlier in the book that may help to mitigate your receipt of junk and spam messages?

- What is the difference between junk and spam messages?

- Why might it not even be worth your time to report spammers and spam messages?

- What is "phishing", and why is it so dangerous and devious?

- What is "spoofing"? Related to this, why do I recommend you not report spammers until you have received multiple spam messages from this same spammer?

- What is "photo spam", and how does it work?

- What is a great keystroke combination to remember to help you with quickly and permanently deleting received junk and spam messages?

Key Strategy Review:

Key Strategy #31: Become ruthless at identifying and deleting possible spam.

Key Strategy #32: Never open a suspicious e-mail attachment.

Key Strategy #33: Use the "Shift-Delete" keystroke combination to bypass your "Deleted Items" folder and knock likely junk/spam e-mails completely out of your account.

Key Strategy #34: Don't click on an embedded URL or web address/hyperlink unless you implicitly trust the sender of the message.

Key Strategy #35: Never enter information into an open box or field in a received e-mail.

Key Strategy #36: "Blacklist" only identified *repeat* spammers.

Key Strategy #37: Unsubscribe or auto-delete junk e-mails versus reporting as spam.

Key Strategy #38: Consider setting up a rule to auto-file e-newsletters and e-zines in an inbox subfolder.

Video Tutorials:

Video Tutorial #9: Using the "rules" options to auto-delete and/or auto-file messages from specific senders.

179

PART IV

**E-mail Strategies for PDA /
Smartphone Users and Additional
Useful E-mail Services / Functions**

CHAPTER 18

Commonsense E-mail Strategies with PDAs and Smartphones, and a Couple Quick Out-of-Office E-mail Strategies

There are a number of devices that have been quite the rage with many business professionals for the last several years, starting with the Palm PDA devices back in the mid to late '90s, and continuing with all of the new iterations of PDA and smartphone devices, including the Pocket PC, BlackBerry, and now the Apple iPhone. A large number of PDAs and smartphones now allow you to wirelessly connect with e-mail and the Internet whenever you are away from the office, giving you accessibility and possible productivity when "on the road."

Obviously, each of these devices has a different manner and way to retrieve, use, and send e-mail, so I'm not going to go into great detail about how to complete very specific tasks or use specific functions or programs within any of them. Each individual PDA or smartphone could have an entire book written just on how to use all of its different functions, programs, and capabilities. Rather than get into that level of detail, I would like to instead share some good commonsense strategies on how you can be more effective and efficient with these devices regardless of which one you are using.

KEY STRATEGY #39
When using a PDA or Smartphone to access e-mail, consider replying to the message by phone versus text.

The first strategy that I'd like to recommend is this: If you receive an e-mail message on your PDA or smartphone and it is a relatively short message—meaning one to which you can give a fairly quick reply—seriously consider whether sending a text/e-mail reply via the device is even the smartest way to respond. You may instead want to simply reply to the message by giving that person a real quick phone call to answer the query. (And, if you are really smart, you'll try to reply at a time when there is a good chance that the person will not even be at his or her desk, so you can just leave a quick voice-mail answer and avoid getting caught in a full conversation!)

The reasoning behind this strategy comes from my personal experience. I have found that I type much faster on a full-size keyboard than on any kind of PDA-device keyboard (ten fingers are almost always faster than two fingers!), and I also know that I can talk much faster than I can type on any keyboard. It just makes a lot of sense to consider not typing or texting a reply message when you can more quickly reply to it by voice. (If you are one of those phenomenal teenage texters, you might be able to respond "by thumbs" more quickly than I can, but if you are a little more "seasoned," as I am, the voice response method certainly can be more efficient.)

A lot of the PDAs and smartphones have a really neat function in them: "embedded intelligence." What this means is that many of these devices can "sense" or identify embedded e-mail addresses and/or telephone numbers in received e-mails, text documents, messages, and/or Web pages visited. For example, if you receive a message that has an e-mail signature at the bottom of the message, very often that signature will include a phone number. Many of the PDA devices I've used are smart enough to identify that phone number, and highlight it. If you then click on that phone number, the device will give you the option to make a call to that number "on the fly" directly from the e-mail, document, or web page. Using this capability can obviously save you even more time if you decide to provide a quick response to an e-mail via telephone. You can call right from the e-mail itself, usually with only one or two clicks of a button – that's efficient!

KEY STRATEGY #40

If you frequently use your PDA or Smart-phone to create and respond to e-mails and/or to create other text-based documents, consider purchasing an external keyboard

The second strategy that I recommend you consider as a PDA and/or smartphone user is this: consider purchasing a full-size external keyboard for your device. If you use a PDA or smartphone very frequently for keeping up with and replying to e-mail messages, and/or if you use the device to create new text or numerical documents—especially if you are out of your office a significant amount of time—consider the possibility of buying either an attachable or wireless-enabled full-size keyboard. Some of these devices attach directly to your PDA or smartphone, often utilizing your charger port. These work fine.

I personally own a very slick Bluetooth-enabled battery-powered wireless keyboard that works with both Palm and Pocket PC devices. As long as my Palm or Pocket PC PDA or smartphone has Bluetooth capability, I do not even have to plug the device into the keyboard—I just have to be in range. The keyboard will pick up the device, and allow me to type at full ten-fingered speed when replying to e-mails and also when creating documents. My keyboard, as well as many of the others on the market, are designed so that they can fold down from a full-size keyboard into a much smaller size— often about the same size as the PDA device itself—for easy packing and travel. These keyboards typically cost anywhere from $50 to $100, but they pay for themselves in gained efficiency and productivity very quickly.

Related to this, remember that these keyboards are handy not just for replying to your e-mail, but also for any text or numerical documents you might create. Many of today's PDAs and smartphones have fully enabled versions of Microsoft Excel and/or Word onboard, or other programs that are equivalent. So you can truly use your full-size keyboard as a very handy way to gain speed and efficiency when utilizing your PDA and smartphone. It may even make it possible for you to save a lot of bulk when you take your next business trip, since you won't have to take along your laptop. All you will need is your PDA, your keyboard, and any electronic files or documents you might need for reference and/or action while on the road. So next time you're out to buy your new PDA or smartphone, or if you just happen to be in your wireless or electronics store (even if that store is online!), ask about the available accessories for your device—especially the keyboard attachment or wireless-enabled keyboard.

KEY STRATEGY #41
Use your PDA/Smartphone to keep on top of junk/spam e-mails.

The third and final commonsense strategy in this chapter is to simply use your PDA or smartphone as a tool to delete junk and spam messages when you're away from your office. Very often, you'll log in to your e-mail account using your PDA or smartphone via some sort of a Web-enabled e-mail server, meaning that you're getting access to the new e-mails that have come into your account since you've been away from your desk. Regardless of whether you receive only your new e-mails via a Web site or have access to your full e-mail account via your PDA/smartphone, I recommend that you consistently and actively use your device as a tool to delete the junk and spam you receive when you are away from your workstation. (This is a great little way to use those five or ten minute pockets of unanticipated "downtime" you run into throughout the day – jump on your smartphone, open your e-mail, and start deleting junk and spam!)

That way, when you get back to your desk, only the e-mails with true business value will be there to greet you. And, you'll be able to go full speed ahead on those e-mails with all ten fingers! The junk and spam will be cleared out of the way, so you can dive right in and start working on real e-mails rather than having to waste time processing junk and spam. Follow this philosophy, and get yourself "down to business" much more quickly when you get back into your office.

Obviously, when you are away from your office and using a PDA and/or smartphone to check your e-mail (and even if you might be checking e-mail via a remote PC or Web terminal), you should follow an abbreviated form of the strategies shared to this point in the book. This means that you should still follow the Three-Minute Rule when at all possible, delete the junk and spam as quickly as possible, and also delete any completed messages that have no retention value. Usually, you will not have the capability to do all of the filing that we have talked about previously, but at least you'll be able to keep your e-mail account cleaner when on the road so that when you get back into your office, all you will face are those messages with true and relevant value, as well as those that need to be filed. You'll be able to get back to productivity much more quickly, and keep your e-mail beast on a leash and under control even when you're not at your desk.

Two Quick Final "Out-of-Office" Strategies

While not specifically related to PDAs and smartphones, here are a couple quick strategies that you can use to help make your time out of the office, and time coming back into the office, more productive and manageable:

KEY STRATEGY #42

Use your e-mail's "Out-of-Office" autoreply function to set reasonable expectations.

Most commercial e-mail tools have an onboard "out-of-office" autoreply capability, and these tools can be very handy for helping to set reasonable expectations with those communicating with you by e-mail. I recommend for you to use your "out-of-office" tool not only when you are out of the office for extended times (vacations, conferences, major business trips, and so on), but also when you might be away from your desk for even just a couple of hours. Let's say you have a lengthy morning meeting planned that will run from 9:00 a.m. to Noon. Why not set up an autoreply telling people that you will be out of the office all morning, and will likely be getting back to people sometime in the afternoon? That way, if they send you something critical and/or urgent, they know you are not available by e-mail and that they may either need to come find you, or that they need to handle it themselves, or that they need to find someone else to work on it. Regardless, you won't feel as much heat because you set appropriate expectations, and you might just see some extra work taken off your plate simply because you let people know you aren't there.

Related to this, has this ever happened to you: Do you ever dread going on a much-needed vacation, simply because you are scared to death of the e-mail mess you'll come back to when the vacation is over? I don't know how many busy professionals have shared this with me, and I always share this simple idea in reply: why not lie just a little when you set up your autoreply before an extended leave from the office? Here's what I mean:

KEY STRATEGY #43

When using your "out-of-office" autoreply to set appropriate expectations, consider "fibbing a little" to buy some extra needed "sanity" time.

Let's say you are leaving on a seven-day vacation, and you know that your e-mail account will be swamped upon your return. Why not set up your autoreply to let people know that you'll actually be out of the office for nine or ten days? Thus, they'll be expecting your replies two to three days later than when you actually return to the office – use those two to three days to get caught up on your e-mails and projects before letting the insanity find you again! Of course, I do recommend that you tell your boss and maybe a couple of other important people how long it is that you'll truly be gone, but keep that list short. Let everyone else think you'll actually be gone ten days – they'll be pleasantly surprised if you end up replying a day or two before they thought you'd be back, and you can use those two to three days of "sanity time" to actually figure out what is truly critical and urgent before letting everyone know you are back.

You could even use this trick on a much shorter time scale: Let's say you have a 2-hour meeting planned from 9:00 a.m. to 11:00 a.m. Why not tell people you'll be out of the office until after lunch, so you actually have that hour from 11:00 to 12:00 to get caught up from the meeting, and deal with any emerging urgency or crises? (You'll probably also greatly increase your chances of actually getting a lunch that day too!) Not a bad idea, eh? Try this little strategy on your next vacation, or even with your next team meeting, and maybe you'll even trick your own e-mail beast a bit!

End of Chapter Review Questions:

- Why is it that I recommend you reply to relatively short, quick e-mail messages received on your smartphone/PDA by voice rather than by text? When is the best time to make those voice replies?

- What useful external tool might be very handy if you are doing significant e-mail and document creation work with your PDA/smartphone?

- What is one of the very best ways to use your PDA/smartphone to keep your account under control when away from the office, especially when you have a five-to-ten minute window of unexpected downtime?

- When should you use your "out of office" autoreply?

• What are a couple ways you can use your "out of office" autoreply function to set more reasonable expectations?

Key Strategy Review:

Key Strategy #39: When using a PDA or Smartphone to access e-mail, consider replying to the message by phone versus text.

Key Strategy #40: If you frequently use your PDA or Smartphone to create and respond to e-mails and/or to create other text-based documents, consider purchasing an external keyboard.

Key Strategy #41: Use your PDA/Smartphone to keep on top of junk/spam e-mails.

Key Strategy #42: Use your e-mail's "Out-of-Office" autoreply function to set reasonable expectations.

Key Strategy #43: When using your "out-of-office" autoreply to set appropriate expectations, consider "fibbing a little" to buy some extra needed "sanity" time.

CHAPTER 19

Group Distribution Lists and Other Useful E-mail Services and Capabilities

In this chapter, I'd like to go beyond the scope of just regular e-mail messaging—messages sent back and forth between two people (two professionals, two colleagues, two friends), and go into the realm of some of the capabilities and tools that are now available due to the increase in broadband access and recent improvements in Web-based software services. There are three or four specific tools that can really jazz up your e-mail capabilities.

KEY STRATEGY #44
Set up useful group distribution lists within your e-mail account.

One of the first tools I'd like to discuss is one that is likely already "embedded" within your commercial or Interned-based e-mail system: the group distribution list. Utilizing group distribution lists can save you quite a bit of time, because you will not have to type in the individual e-mail addresses of everyone in a group of people to whom you regularly send messages (say, for instance, the people in your department at work, the people on your project team, a small group of close friends, the members of your neighborhood community association, and so on). Having a group distribution list will probably save you a few seconds to maybe a minute every time you send a message to the group. That may not seem like a lot of time if you look at it on the basis of an individual message, but if you add up all the time that you will save over a year (or even a twenty- to thirty-year career), you'll understand the value of group distribution lists.

Here's how to set up a group distribution list in Microsoft Outlook:

1. First, create a new message by clicking on the "New Message" button in Outlook's e-mail tool

2. Then, click on the "To" button once the new message box is opened

3. Next, click on the "New" button once the "Select Names" pop-up screen opens

4. Then, select "New Distribution List" when the "New Entry" pop-up screen opens

5. Next, select the desired members from your Contacts list. (Note: If any of the people you desire to add to this e-mail distribution list are not in your Contacts list, you have to add them to your Contacts to also add them to your new distribution list. You can add such names to your Contacts database while creating the distribution list.)

6. Once you have all desired distribution list members and their appropriate e-mails identified and added, type in the desired name of the new distribution list, and hit "Save and Close."

7. From this point forward, whenever you need to send a message to this group, you simply need to type the name of the distribution list in the "To" field of any new e-mail,

and the full set of e-mail addresses will auto-populate the field. (Note: You also can hit the "To" button, and scroll through the list of Contacts to find the distribution list—it will be in bold with a little group icon in front of it, which signifies a group distribution list.)

This obviously is a good time for a video tutorial on how to set up and use a group distribution list:

Video Tutorial #10: *Setting up a group distribution list in Microsoft Outlook.*

Video Tutorial #11: *Setting up a group distribution list in Yahoo! Mail.*

Remember to visit the Taming E-mail Reader web site at: http://www.tamingemailreader.com/videotutorials.html to see this and all of the other related video tutorials from *Taming the E-mail Beast.*

I recommend that you set up personal and professional group distribution lists for every group of people you expect to send messages to more than once. By the third or fourth time you send each of these groups a message, you'll have saved the time it takes to set up the group distribution list. From that point forward, you are saving time big time every time you mail a message to that group! (But don't use this tool to make it easy for you to simply send too many CC/FYI messages to your team – remember Chapters 13 and 14?)

If you send promotional/informational e-mails to large audiences, consider a commercial e-mail distribution service

While small group distribution lists are very useful for sending to small, repeating audiences, they are not terribly functional if you want to send e-mails to hundreds if not thousands of individuals. Most standard commercial e-mail programs have a cutoff on the number of people you can send a message to, and, if you are sending to hundreds of people (or more), sending an impersonal message with a generic greeting always lessens effectiveness. Several business professionals I know (myself included!)—and thousands of other like-minded individuals throughout the United States and abroad—use e-mail as a "power tool" to more effectively share information about their companies and also to market the products and services of their companies or organizations. We're not talking spam or junk here—we are instead talking about "opt-in/permission-based" e-mail communications.

Opt in e-mail lists are e-mail services to which you "subscribe" in order to receive future information from a desired sender. For instance, every month I send out an e-mail e-zine called "Timely Tips" to a reader list of more than 2,500 people (Timely Tips provides a single time-saving tip each month, covering both business and personal areas of life.) Each of these individuals signed up for my Timely Tips e-newsletter by registering through my Web site, sending me an e-mail request, or asking to be added to my newsletter at one of my conference speaking programs or corporate/organizational training sessions. When people ask you for information, the e-mail you send to them is obviously not junk or spam—it is instead often a valuable service. If you provide information to a permission-based list—any kind of subscription-based e-mail message, newsletter, e-zine, product update, and so on—you may want to consider using one of the many available commercial permission-based e-mail services.

For a few years now, I have been utilizing a subscription service called Constant Contact (*www.constantcontact. com*). This well-designed tool allows you to send individual, personalized HTML-formatted e-mails with nice graphics, pictures, and text that are very easy to develop. Every message you send through this service starts out with "Dear <Name>," with the name being the first name of each subscriber on your list, thus adding a very professional *and* personal touch to each message. With this service you actually create a single generic e-mail message, but set it up so that there is a field that will auto-populate each recipient's name from your database, thereby personalizing the message to each specific person. Because this is a permission-based tool, everyone who receives the message must have given express permission at some point in the past for you to send him or her information via e-mail.

In addition to enabling me to easily send professionally formatted, personalized e-mails, Constant Contact also allowed me to fully upload and import my subscription database from a file on my PC—meaning I did not have to "hand enter" information for every single person in my list. I can also add new subscribers at any time using the same import/upload capability, or use an easy "wizard" tool if I only want to put in one or two new subscribers. Also, Constant Contact—as well as most other legitimate permission-based e-mail tools—actually requires you to provide an "Unsubscribe" option with every e-mail that you send, so if people determine they no longer want your e-mails, they can easily stop getting them.

Of course, you want to make sure that your list is truly permission-based, because if it isn't, using a tool like this makes you no better than the average spammer that we've talked so negatively about earlier in the book, and may actually put you at some criminal or litigation risk. New laws passed in recent years have really focused on illicit spam messages and the senders behind them. Sending e-mail without permission is neither a good nor ethical way to build your business, so resist the temptation. (Constant Contact will actually knock you out of its system if you break its permission-based bylaws.)

The Commercial E-mail Auto-Responder

This is another very handy commercial e-mail tool, which is similar, but much more sophisticated, than the "out-of-office" autoreply tool that many professionals already use. An auto-responder is a software tool that basically allows you to have an automated message "reply" to any person submitting information via a Web page submission form, or in an e-mail sent to a specific e-mail address.

Let's first clarify that an auto-responder is not the same as an auto-reply. For example, everyone who sends a message to *custom@randalldean.com* gets an automated reply that provides the original sender with information that ideally will help them along to the next stage in whatever information they seek or action they want to take.

Rather than having to send an individualized reply to each query generated from a specific account or web page submission, you can set up an auto-reply with a generic response that is intended to provide the sender with needed information—perhaps a FAQ list that answers the questions senders are likely to ask, or gives them information on how to complete an order, or what they need to know to properly request services or ask questions. Obviously, the "out-of-office" feature in your e-mail account is perhaps the most-used form of the auto-reply function, and you can definitely utilize your out-of-office tool as your auto-reply tool in many circumstances.

This is especially true with an e-mail account that is not designated to a specific person but is instead set up to simply provide a generic reply to incoming messages. Many organizations even use a "Do Not Reply" e-mail address (for example, *DoNotReply@randalldean.com*), because this specifically tells any receiver that any reply they send to this message will just continue to get the auto-reply message. But the typical autoreply function in most e-mail programs is a fairly simplistic tool.

A true auto-responder is a slightly different beast. An auto-responder is a software tool that typically allows you to set up a message that will be sent automatically when a person submits personal information, a request for information, or sends a question via an Internet-based query. The auto-responder tool will then send a specified message—or possibly even a designated *series* of messages— to the original requester to facilitate appropriate information sharing, relationship development, and possibly prospect-to-client conversion. Many organizations utilize these tools to take generic new prospects into their database and make sure that these prospects get an appropriate level of information for them to move the relationship forward, with the goal of ultimately converting these prospects into paying clients over a designated time frame.

Here's an example: Let's say that I submit my personal information to a Web site that offers time management strategies and related products, as well as client consultation and on-site training programs. To help facilitate the development of my relationship with this firm, the firm uses a commercial auto-responder tool that not only "submits" my information into their prospect database, but also then sends a series of messages—typically anywhere from two to seven messages (although it could be many more than seven)—each of which provides me with useful information about this firm. Each message will have a different topic or theme, and each message will have a different "action" or goal related to it for the recipient/submitter, with an ultimate goal of prospect-to-client conversion at the end of the process (in other words, the company wants me to eventually purchase products and/or services rather than simply request information).

Obviously, these tools work better when they are a fully integrated segment of a multiple-medium marketing/sales strategy—thus, in addition to getting the auto-responder e-mails, the submitter also get a full information packet in the mail, as well as a phone call from a client development representative and possibly an invitation to an in-person meeting—but even an auto-responder set up by itself can do some amazing things related to converting identified prospects to paying clients.

It does take a little bit of skill from both the marketing and communications perspective and the software user/ IT perspective to properly set up an auto-responder. You typically have to learn how to utilize the functionality of the auto-responder service or program that you're using, and you also have to learn how to write a good series of messages that answers the questions that people may have, provides the information that will help facilitate the development of the relationship either as a client or as a prospect, and/or ideally will get them to take a desired action. It truly is a somewhat sophisticated marketing/sales communication tool, and one that anyone with an Internet presence should strongly consider learning and using. If you can properly set up one of these auto-responder tools, you'll save your company and client/sales team a great amount of time and energy, as well as increase the business-building potential with your clients and with your prospects. It is definitely a tool worth considering for any organization actively pursuing sales, marketing, prospect development, and/or client retention.

For a little over a year now I have been using a tool called AWeber, which is an excellently designed auto-responder that has recently been significantly upgraded to make it easier to use. You can easily set up a "squeeze page" on your Web site that is connected to AWeber. Whenever someone submits his or her personal information and/or request for company information on this "squeeze page," AWeber automatically contacts the appropriate client manager with the new prospect's information (so that person can be added to a database/call list), and also starts up the defined auto-responder series of follow-up messages. Then, the requester will start to receive appropriately timed messages to provide useful information about the company that will (it is hoped) advance the relationship from simple prospect to long-term client.

As the user of the auto-responder, all you have to do is set up the messages one time (with obvious care and forethought), and then the service will send an appropriate series of personalized messages to each and every requester moving forward. Obviously, this can save significant time compared to sending individual personalized replies to each and every person submitting information via your Web site, or each person submitting a question/request for information to an open e-mail account. To find more information about this product, go to http://www.aweber.com. (Another autoresponder tool worth mentioning is http://www.1shoppingcart.com – they tie together e-mail autoresponders with other sophisticated e-commerce tools for just about any size firm looking to do business via e-mail and the web.) Both of these services/tools are very useful for enhancing the quality and profitability of your Internet and e-mail presence.

Other "Cool" E-mail Tools

There are also some available services that can enhance promotional-based e-mail communications from a customer or client relationship perspective, or prospect-enticement perspective. You can now create e-mails that allow your recipient to click on a link and either get a voice or video message—and you can even personalize these messages to a specific individual if you so choose.

One of the audio tools that I'm aware of is called Audio Generator, which has been developed by leading Internet marketers Armand Morin and Alex Mandossian, and some of their business partners (*www.AudioGenerator.com*). For a monthly service fee, you can create audio messages that can be linked to via e-mail or on a Web page, and that can be launched by anyone receiving the e-mail or visiting the Web page. Rather than receiving only a text-only message, visitors now can hear a warm and welcoming voice greeting them. It is just one way to enhance their experience and facilitate the development of the relationship with a new prospect or existing client.

Another tool now available also allows you to send an e-mail message that links to a video-streaming server, which will allow you to create and send personalized messages in video format to your customers or clients. All you need is a good webcam and appropriate Internet bandwidth, and/or a solid digital video camera, and with these simple tools, you can create short *personalized* video messages for prospective clients or customers. You create the message, post it to the video server, and then add the link to this streaming video to the body text of your e-mail (or even embed the video right into the message!) All that the recipients or Web visitors need to do is click this link to launch the video message (or, in the case of embedded video, just open the message!) Then, the receiver gets not only the warmth of voice, but also the full scope of the communications experience—voice plus visual! They can both see you and hear you—a tool that can truly make the relationship feel that much closer. One service I know of that provides this tool is *www.HelloWorld.com*, although I believe there are many others also available.

Obviously, we've shared a number of tools here, many of which will help you perform better and more efficiently from the marketing, communications, and prospect/client development perspective. On the *Taming the E-mail Beast* book reader's Web site (*www.tamingemailreader.com*), I've provided all of these links for easy access, so that you can review each of these tools, look at the pros and cons, and make a decision for yourself about whether or not they are right for you and/or your organization. If you have created or improved your company's Internet presence and profitability, or plan to do so, these e-mail–related tools can go a long way toward helping you achieve your goals in an efficient and effective manner.

End of Chapter Review Questions:

- What is an e-mail group distribution list? How can it save you time and enhance productivity?

- What is the difference between a group distribution list and a commercial e-mail distribution service?

- What is the difference between a simply autoreply (such as "out of office") and a commercial e-mail Autoresponder service?

- What are some examples of e-mail and web-based tools that allow you to integrate voice and even video into your messages?

Key Strategy Review:

Key Strategy #44: Set up useful group distribution lists within your e-mail account.

Video Tutorials:

Video Tutorial #10: *Setting up a group distribution list in Microsoft Outlook.*

Video Tutorial #11: *Setting up a group distribution list in Yahoo! Mail.*

CHAPTER 20

Share These Strategies!

So there you have it! A full set of strategies that will help you administer your e-mail account efficiently, effectively, and professionally. If you follow even just a few of the strategies that we've shared in this book, you are going to be a significantly more efficient and effective e-mail communicator. You're also going to be significantly more efficient and effective at managing your time and gaining productivity, because that is what these strategies are really all about. I hope that you have already begun to utilize your e-mail in a more proactive manner and much less reactively, so that you can be more focused on the most important priorities in your work and in your life, rather than the new "crisis du jour" that just came in via your e-mail. I am quite confident that the strategies shared in this book will greatly help you to accomplish more, not only in your e-mail administration, but also in your work and your life. Hopefully, by following these strategies, you will once and for all *tame your e-mail beast.*

It is now time for the final key strategy:

KEY STRATEGY #45
Share these strategies!

Obviously, this book contains many good ideas for more effective e-mail management. And, of course, they will work for you even if you are the only one who uses them. But think about the possible benefits of these strategies if they were shared a little bit more widely, perhaps with your work team, or department, or even your entire company or organization (or how about just with your family and friends?) Think about how much more that could help you personally and professionally, as well as how much more that could help them.

Let's give this some thought: Are there members of your work team or your personal/professional contacts who have exhibited some of the bad habits described earlier in the book? Are there people you know who are actively *blinging* every day? Are there people on your team who constantly overuse carbon copy? Are there people who don't give enough additional information when they reply to or forward messages? Are there people constantly getting caught in those *e-mail insanity loops*?

Are there people in your circle who let their e-mail inbox get so cluttered up with hundreds (if not thousands) of messages that they lose significant time every day searching for the messages they need, and also miss responses that need to be made in a timely manner? Do these same people reread many of their already completed or tasked messages over and over, thus losing significant productivity and time every single day? Do you know people (yourself included!) who receive way too many messages from friends? Or get too many junk and spam messages because they are utilizing their professional account for too many purposes, making it both accessible and susceptible to getting added to those spam and junk e-mail lists?

If you see any of these things happening frequently in your workplace, or if you have family and friends who you know are struggling with effective and proper management of their e-mail, then share these strategies! I know this is a shameless plug—but how expensive is it to get every single person on your list a copy of this book? (It would really make a great holiday or birthday present for just about any struggling e-mailer in your life!) And, if you see these behaviors damaging your company's productivity, morale, and effectiveness, you might even consider bringing in an expert (like me!) to lead a training program on this topic, and get every single person on your team to operate within the same philosophy and strategies.

Think about the possibilities of having your entire work team operating with these principles. You would receive fewer e-mail firebombs, fewer CC e-mails that you didn't need to receive, more concise e-mails with more specific information about related tasks and deliverables, and less junk and spam (which would also reduce the risk of downloading viruses, spyware or adware.)

If you are a manager or leader in your organization, you'd find that the team members who report to you likely would become more productive, and/or achieve better work-life balance (hopefully both!) You would see people more likely to respond quickly to short little e-mails, because they would be following the Three-Minute Rule (not to mention that they would be caught up with their e-mails in the first place, thus increasing both their timeliness and responsiveness). Thus work wouldn't get backed up—it would flow properly and without any unnecessary blockages. Stress would go down and productivity would go up—not just for you, but for the people around you. All of these things are the possible benefits of sharing these strategies.

The benefits of following a smart and intelligent e-mail management system can only be multiplied when they are shared across an entire team of users. You might even petition to make this book standard reading for your company or organization, or part of your new-hire training program. Share this book with your HR/training manager and see if he or she might make it standard corporate reading, or possibly part of the new employee manual, or something the company will distribute to the members of your work team or department. See if you can get these strategies spread around your entire organization so that you're not the only sane e-mailer in your organization. (Who wants to be surrounded by a bunch of "crazies"?) Instead, make a smart effort to get surrounded by a whole group of people that are using their e-mail in a smart, intelligent, and proactive manner, and you'll personally receive a significant benefit.

I would bet that it is not outside the realm of possibility that you might realize anywhere from a 10 to 30 percent decrease in your flow of e-mail (or more!) by adopting these strategies, and also by getting the other people around you to adopt them too, because of the synergistic benefit you get from multiple people following the same set of strategies. It behooves you personally to take a look at trying to make this happen. It might even make you a champion in your organization! You will greatly enhance your productivity and your sanity when you not only get your own e-mail beast tamed, but when you help others get their e-mail beasts tamed too.

In closing, I do hope that you found the strategies, techniques, and philosophies shared in this book valuable, and that they will give you the opportunity to get your e-mail back under control, and also get your e-mail back to being the powerful functional tool for personal and business productivity it was meant to be. It no longer needs to be that reactive urgency-creator that drains your energy, motivation, and capability to effectively accomplish your work. It can be something better – it can be something more.

I wish you all the best in your future e-mailing endeavors and would love to hear from you regarding your success following these strategies (*randy@randalldean.com*). Good luck now and forever with your newly tamed e-mail beast!

> *"Be the change you wish to see in the world."*
> -Gandhi

> *"Be the change you wish to see in your e-mail account."*
> -Randy Dean
> The E-mail Sanity Expert

End of Chapter Review Question:

- What one thing will you do right now, at the end of reading this book, to help others get their e-mail beasts tamed and under control?

Key Strategy Review:

Key Strategy #45: Share these strategies!

APPENDICES

Appendix A: 45 Key Strategies for Better Managing Your E-mail Overload

Appendix B: Full List of Video Tutorials from *Taming the E-mail Beast*

Appendix C: Full List of End of Chapter Questions

More on the Author: *Randy Dean*

APPENDIX A

45 Key Strategies for Better Managing Your E-mail Overload

CHAPTER 1

Key Strategy #1: To understand the size of your e-mail beast, track the number of e-mails you receive, and the time you spend on them

CHAPTER 2

Key Strategy #2: Have at least three e-mail accounts

CHAPTER 3

Key Strategy #3: Follow the three-minute, one-touch rule

CHAPTER 4

Key Strategy #4: Prioritize e-mails (and related tasks) that take more than three minutes

Key Strategy #5: Use "Drag & Drop" to create new tasks from your e-mails, then file related e-mails in your "Priority Processing" folder

CHAPTER 5

Key Strategy #6: Get into the habit of only checking your e-mail account at a few designated times per day

CHAPTER 6

Key Strategy #7: Don't Bling! (Don't constantly check your e-mail throughout the day.)

CHAPTER 7

Key Strategy #8: Create a personalized e-mail file folder infrastructure

Key Strategy #9: When using a folder/subfolder e-mail filing system, Keep it Simple (Stupid!)

CHAPTER 8

Key Strategy #10: Set a goal to get your professional e-mail account's inbox down to ZERO messages at least once per week.

Key Strategy #11: Get ruthless and quick at filing "completed" messages, and also at creating new folders for those messages if no good folder exists. *(Corollary: Don't keep rereading completed messages!)*

CHAPTER 9

Key Strategy #12: When cleaning up hundreds or even thousands of legacy e-mails, sacrifice some accuracy for speed by using the "sort" function embedded in your e-mail software to mass-file and mass-delete messages.

Key Strategy #13: Learn what your company's formal document and e-document (including e-mail) retention policies are, and follow them. If they do not exist, press your legal staff/counsel to research and develop appropriate policies for your organization.

CHAPTER 10

Key Strategy #14: Once you get your e-mail account clean, don't EVER let it get re-cluttered and disorganized

Key Strategy #15: Set a personal maximum to the number of e-mails you will allow to gather in your professional account

CHAPTER 11

Key Strategy #16: Learn how to use your e-mail system's embedded "Search" tool.

CHAPTER 12

Key Strategy #17: Learn how to properly set up and use your primary e-mail's archival function

Key Strategy #18: Consider setting up the auto archive properties immediately upon the creation of any new folder or subfolder.

CHAPTER 13

Key Strategy #19: End the FYI/"Just Thought You'd Want to Know" e-mails.

Key Strategy #20: Consider only forwarding or CC'ing messages in which all recipients have a defined task or action to complete.

Key Strategy #21: Consider deleting unnecessary historical text when forwarding or replying to messages.

Key Strategy #22: Change the subject line text when the subject changes.

Key Strategy #23: Stop the insanity of unproductive e-mail loops.

CHAPTER 14

Key Strategy #24: Never CC or forward to a group of people an e-mail that contains an open task with no defined "owner".

Key Strategy #25: Remember that diffused responsibility for an e-mail–related task really means *no* responsibility.

Key Strategy #26: Identify those using "CC as a CYA" and encourage them (mandate for them?) to follow a more sensible e-mail CC/forwarding philosophy.

CHAPTER 15

Key Strategy #27: When you receive an e-mail firebomb, *don't panic*!

Key Strategy #28: Before handing off any important e-mail, including those carrying a potential crisis, verify that the person being handed the e-mail accepts and agrees to take ownership and responsibility for the e-mail and any embedded tasks/deliverables.

CHAPTER 16

Key Strategy #29: In every communications situation, consider whether or not e-mail is the most efficient and/or effective communication method.

Key Strategy #30: Never forget about the other technology-enabled communications tools that might be better options for a given interpersonal communications situation.

CHAPTER 17

Key Strategy #31: Become Ruthless at Identifying and Deleting Possible Spam.

Key Strategy #32: Never open a suspicious e-mail

attachment.

Key Strategy #33: Use the "Shift-Delete" keystroke combination to bypass your "Deleted Items" folder and knock likely junk/spam e-mails completely out of your account.

Key Strategy #34: Don't click on an embedded URL or web address/hyperlink unless you implicitly trust the sender of the message.

Key Strategy #35: Never enter information into an open box or field in a received e-mail.

Key Strategy #36: "Blacklist" only identified *repeat* spammers.

Key Strategy #37: Unsubscribe or auto-delete junk e-mails versus reporting as spam.

Key Strategy #38: Consider setting up a rule to auto-file e-newsletters and e-zines in an inbox subfolder.

CHAPTER 18

Key Strategy #39: When using a PDA or Smartphone to access e-mail, consider replying to the message by phone versus text.

Key Strategy #40: If you frequently use your PDA or Smartphone to create and respond to e-mails and/or to create other text-based documents, consider purchasing an external keyboard.

Key Strategy #41: Use your PDA/Smartphone to keep on top of junk/spam e-mails.

Key Strategy #42: Use your e-mail's "Out-of-Office" autoreply function to set reasonable expectations.

Key Strategy #43: When using your "out-of-office" autoreply to set appropriate expectations, consider "fibbing a little" to buy some extra needed "sanity" time.

CHAPTER 19

Key Strategy #44: Set up useful group distribution lists within your e-mail account.

CHAPTER 20

Key Strategy #45: Share these strategies!

APPENDIX B

Full List of Video Tutorials

CHAPTER 4

<u>Video Tutorial #1:</u> *Printing E-mails and Filing in Your Priority File*

<u>Video Tutorial #2:</u> *Creating a new "Priority Processing" folder in your e-mail's inbox, and integrating related e-mail tasks into your task list*

<u>Video Tutorial #3:</u> *Using "Drag & Drop" to create a task, calendar item, a new contact, and/or new note/memo in your PIM program*

CHAPTER 7

<u>Video Tutorial #4:</u> *Creating a new electronic file folder in MS Outlook and Yahoo!(and moving messages from your inbox into an e-mail file folder).*

CHAPTER 9

<u>Video Tutorial #5:</u> *How to mass-select groups of messages and move them into appropriate file folders, using left-clicks, the Shift key (and the "Ctrl" key for noncontiguous e-mails), and drag & drop.*

<u>Video Tutorial #6:</u> *How to sort messages by sender, subject, and/or date in MS Outlook.*

CHAPTER 11

Video Tutorial #7: *Using the e-mail "Search" tool to find a missing message.*

CHAPTER 12

Video Tutorial #8: *Setting up your Auto Archive general settings, and also your AutoArchive properties for individual folders within your e-mail inbox structure.*

CHAPTER 17

Video Tutorial #9: *Using the "rules" options to auto-delete and/or auto-file messages from specific senders.*

CHAPTER 19

Video Tutorial #10: *Setting up a group distribution list in Microsoft Outlook.*

Video Tutorial #11: *Setting up a group distribution list in Yahoo! Mail.*

Remember to visit the Taming E-mail Reader web site at: http://www.tamingemailreader.com/videotutorials.html to see this and all of the other related video tutorials from *Taming the E-mail Beast.*

APPENDIX C

Full List of End of Chapter Questions

INTRODUCTION

- How long have we been using e-mail?

- How much time does the average user spend per day reading and responding to e-mails?

- What makes e-mail such a powerful tool for potential productivity?

- Why has e-mail become an area of "pain" for many users and professionals?

CHAPTER 1

- Why is it important to track and analyze your personal and professional e-mail activities?

- What is the smart thing to do right now if you identify some "e-mail no brainers"?

- What is the Hawthorne Effect, and how can it have a positive impact on your e-mail habits and behaviors?

CHAPTER 2

- What are the three recommended types of e-mail accounts most people should have?

- What are the two key reasons you do you not want to give

your family and friends your work e-mail address?

- Why is the "internet/e-commerce" e-mail account important for maintaining productivity and focus?

- When are two times to consider going beyond three e-mail accounts?

- When is e-mail not the "problem", but the "symptom" of something much larger?

CHAPTER 3

- What is the three-minute, one-touch rule?

- Why do professionals often end up under piles of clutter in their office and e-mail?

- How can following the three-minute, one-touch rule enhance personal and organizational speed and productivity?

- What is a "dead-log" manager?

- What is one strategy to consider doing right now? (Could you put the book down and get started?)

CHAPTER 4

- What is the proper thing to do with e-mails that have embedded tasks that will take longer than three minutes?

- What is the prescribed "old-fashioned" paper-based option?

- How can you do basically the same thing using a "paperless" option that utilizes the functionality of your

PIM program?

- What is a "PIM" program? What are some popular examples of these programs? What kinds of functions do they typically provide?

- What is "drag & drop"? What are two examples of how drag & drop can save time when administering e-mails and related tasks/activities?

CHAPTER 5

- Why is it important to not constantly check your e-mail?

- What are the four recommended times per day for most professionals to check their e-mail?

- Why is it important to have programmed time for effective response to newly received e-mails (30-60 minutes before lunch and before leaving)?

- When are two other flexible times you can check your e-mail without negatively affecting productivity and performance?

- Why is it important to push back on organizations and systems that have adopted a "culture of urgency"?

- How do you adjust the recommended strategy if you are an intensive client/customer service agent?

- What is an "urgency boss"? What is an effective recommended strategy for "managing this manager" related to "urgency bomb" e-mails?

CHAPTER 6

- What is "blinging"?

- Why is blinging such a negative habit for sustained productivity and focus?

- How many IQ points do you lose when you are actively blinging?

- Why is e-mail considered an "open loop" form of communication? And why is it important to follow through on urgent and important e-mails that you send to others?

- What is the recommended advice to follow when dealing with a "blinging" boss?

CHAPTER 7

- What is the key reason that you want to build a file "infrastructure" for your e-mail account?

- What does K.I.S.S. stand for? Why is it relevant when building and administering an e-mail filing infrastructure?

- How do you best handle e-mails that might have "split personalities"?

- What is a possible longer-term way to think about the development of your e-mail filing infrastructure?

CHAPTER 8

- What is the first critical step necessary to start an effective e-mail cleanup process?

- What is the "pain" involved with an e-mail cleanup process?

- Once you complete your initial e-mail inbox cleanup process, what should now be your weekly goal related to your e-mail account?

- What is the difference between a "completed" e-mail and an "active" e-mail?

- Why is rereading "completed" e-mails so damaging to productivity?

- How do you convert an "active" e-mail into a "completed" e-mail?

CHAPTER 9

- What is it that you have to sacrifice in order to clean up hundreds or even thousands of inbox messages in a reasonably quick and efficient manner?

- What embedded tool in most commercial e-mail software programs helps to facilitate an efficient clean-up process?

- What is the recommended thing to do with old e-mails – especially those with potential litigation risk – in the absence of a formal document retention policy?

- Why is a formal document/e-document retention policy so helpful for keeping individual e-mail accounts clean?

- Who should be responsible for developing your company's formal document/e-document retention policy? Why?

CHAPTER 10

- Why is it important to keep your professional e-mail account "under control" once you've taken the effort to get it to "zero"?

- When does your professional e-mail account become "Priority #1" on your daily to-do list?

- Why is it more important to manage your professional e-mail account more "tightly" than your personal account?

CHAPTER 11

- What is the rationale behind the "File Nothing" e-mail management counter theory?

- How can this theory actually help you be more confident when filing your e-mail messages?

- Why do I file virtually nothing in my Sent Items folder?

- What two embedded tools in your e-mail software are most helpful for finding misplaced messages?

CHAPTER 12

- What are the two key reasons for setting up and using an e-mail archive?

- When is the very best time to set up the auto-archiving properties for any of your folders in your active e-mail account?

- In a corporate/organizational setting, why is it important to consult with your IT staff prior to creating and using an e-mail archive?

CHAPTER 13

- What is the problem with lengthy "FYI/Just thought you'd want to know?" e-mails?

- What is a simple solution to help end the overuse of CC'd and forwarded e-mails?

- What are two compelling reasons to delete the unnecessary "historical text" from forwarded messages?

- What is an "unproductive e-mail loop"? What is a simple solution for ending this "e-mail loop?"

CHAPTER 14

- Why is it that so many people use e-mail "CC as a CYA"?

- What is "diffused responsibility" when related to e-mails and the tasks embedded within them?

- Who should ultimately own the responsibility for a task that doesn't get completed due to "diffused responsibility"?

- When someone on your team sends out too many "CC/FYI" messages, what can you do to help your team regain e-mail sanity?

CHAPTER 15

- What is an "e-mail firebomb"?

- What is the first thing you need to keep yourself from doing when you receive an e-mail firebomb?

- When handing off an e-mail firebomb to someone else, what is the first critical thing you need to verify with that person?

- What is one communications option to never forget when faced with an e-mail firebomb, or any other critical communications/workplace/interpersonal challenge or crisis?

CHAPTER 16

- When is e-mail often the worst form of communications tool to use in a given interpersonal communications situation?

- What are two other highly preferred communications options to remember when dealing with confusing, emotional, or complex communications situations?

- What are some other technology-enabled communications options to remember when facing these interpersonal communications situations?

CHAPTER 17

- Why is spam both so common and so pervasive (think financial!)?

- What are a couple key strategies we've already shared earlier in the book that may help to mitigate your receipt of junk and spam messages?

- What is the difference between junk and spam messages?

- Why might it not even be worth your time to report spammers and spam messages?

- What is "phishing", and why is it so dangerous and devious?

- What is "spoofing"? Related to this, why do I recommend you not report spammers until you have received multiple spam messages from this same spammer?

- What is "photo spam", and how does it work?

- What is a great keystroke combination to remember to help you with quickly and permanently deleting received junk and spam messages?

CHAPTER 18

- Why is it that I recommend you reply to relatively short, quick e-mail messages received on your smartphone/PDA by voice rather than by text? When is the best time to make those voice replies?

- What useful external tool might be very handy if you are doing significant e-mail and document creation work with your PDA/smartphone?

- What is one of the very best ways to use your PDA/smartphone to keep your account under control when away from the office, especially when you have a five-to-ten minute window of unexpected downtime?

- When should you use your "out of office" autoreply?

- What are a couple ways you can use your "out of office" autoreply function to set more reasonable expectations?

CHAPTER 19

- What is an e-mail group distribution list? How can it save you time and enhance productivity?

- What is the difference between a group distribution list and a commercial e-mail distribution service?

- What is the difference between a simply autoreply (such as "out of office") and a commercial e-mail Autoresponder service?

- What are some examples of e-mail and web-based tools that allow you to integrate voice and even video into your messages?

CHAPTER 20

- What one thing will you do right now, at the end of reading this book, to help others get their e-mail beasts tamed and under control?

ABOUT RANDALL DEAN

Randy Dean, known nationally and abroad as the "Totally Obsessed" Time Management Guy and E-mail Sanity Expert, has more than 18 years of experience both using and teaching advanced time management/personal organization systems and strategies. He has personally tested his time management strategies and the related use of appropriate technology, tools, and software in major corporate, academic, and non-profit settings, as well as in two small, fast-paced for-profit companies. He has found that his systems work in just about any professional setting, with enough flexibility to perform in these widely varying environments.

For the last three years, Randy has put a majority of his focus on the effective use and administration of e-mail systems and software, after becoming aware of the growing frustration and angst many professionals were reporting related to their daily use of e-mail. This focus turned into several popular speaking and training programs that have been delivered at several regional and national conferences, major corporations, government entities, and major universities, including opportunities to share this information with international audiences. His strategies work, with many professionals reporting great success at getting their e-mail inbox from hundreds and even thousands of messages all the way down to almost zero.

Randy is also a very popular national speaker and trainer on time management strategies, including the use of related technology systems, including PDA and smartphone devices and also the extended use of Microsoft Outlook. He has several corporate, conference, and major university clients that have become consistent repeat clients, thus showing his capable performance as a speaker and trainer – being both highly informative and engaging in his programs (including a nice touch of humor.) Prior to starting Randall Dean Consulting and Training, LLC, Randy held several impressive professional positions, including time as a market research supervisor in the corporate headquarters at Procter & Gamble, the director of MBA admissions for Michigan State University's Eli Broad Graduate School of Management, and subscriber and circulation services coordinator for the Fetzer Institute. Randy graduated from Western Michigan University with honors in 1991, and was honored as the top graduate of the Broad MBA Program at Michigan State University in 1997. He is an active member of the National Speakers Association and American Society for Training and Development. He is the author of one other time management-related book, Major Satisfactors = Major Success: A Unique New Way to Look at How We All Spend, Use, and Waste Our Time, available on www.randalldean. com, www.amazon.com, and www.barnesandnoble.com.

Some of Randy's most popular conference programs include:

- *Finding An Extra Hour Every Day:* Time Management Tips and Tricks for Busy Managers, Leaders, and Professionals

- *Taming the E-mail Beast:* Key Strategies for Better Managing Your E-mail Overload

Randy also has several more in-depth training programs that he provides for organizations large and small:

- Advanced Time Management and Personal Organization Strategies for Managers and Professionals *(1/2 to Full Day)*

- *Taming the E-mail and Information Overload Beast:* Key Strategies for Better Managing Your E-mail

Overload and Getting Your Office Clutter Under Control *(1/2 day)*

- *Optimizing Your MS Outlook:* Advanced Time Management Strategies for MS Outlook Users

- *The PDA Power Program:* Time Management and Personal Productivity Strategies for PDA and Smartphone Users

- Managing and Leading Great Staff and Team Meetings

- Powerful Presentations and PowerPoint

Following this book, Randy plans to bring out a series of additional e-mail and time management related information products, including audiobooks, podcasts, and formal DVD-based training programs.

To learn more about Randy and his products, programs, and services, visit his web sites:

- http://www.randalldean.com

- http://www.emailsanityexpert.com

- http://www.timely-tips.blogspot.com

Randy also has a specific web site for readers of Taming the E-mail Beast with additional information, resources, and related video tutorials: http://www.tamingemailreader.com.

A few comments from Randy's program attendees:

"Thank you so much Randy for this information! I am now a disciple of your system!! I was able to reduce my inbox from 258 e-mails to 3. I feel like I have climbed Mt. Rushmore!!"

"Randy's enthusiasm and excitement will make you want to apply his principles immediate. You won't regret his workshops."

"The subject matter of this course could prove to be the single greatest improvement in my professional office practices and procedures."

"One of the best courses I have attended – great instructor!"

If you work for an organization that would like to broadly distribute this publication among its employees, or are a member of a membership organization or association that would like to offer this publication to your membership (possibly as a fundraiser), we can provide quantity discounts that can bring down the per unit pricing of this publication dramatically. We can even discuss options where in-person training or speaking programs led by Randy Dean and the distribution of this book can be co-bundled for your employees or members.

If either of these options are of interest, please contact Randall Dean Consulting & Training, LLC at tamingemail@randalldean.com, or call 517-896-6611 for more information.

Index

A

Adware 167-168, 205
Allen, David ii, iv, 28, 30, 42
AOL ix, 55,
Archive/Auto Archive 99, 101, 121-127, 211, 222-223
Attachment 167-168, 177, 179, 185, 213
Autoreply 187-190, 196-197, 201, 213, 225-226
Autoresponder 199, 201, 226
AWeber 199

B

BCC/ Blind Carbon Copies 20
BlackBerry 182
Blacklist 172, 177, 179, 213
Bling/Blinging 9, 55-62, 109, 137, 204, 210, 220

C

CC/Carbon Copies 129-148, 193, 205, 211-212, 223
Cleanup Strategies 80-105
Client/Customer Service 49-50, 54, 60, 75, 219
Commercial E-mail Systems 69
Communications 15, 57, 157
Conversation 156-157, 159, 161

D

Dean, Randall F. 227
Delete/ Deletion 82, 97-99, 169, 173, 177, 179, 213
Document Retention 98-105, 127, 221
"Drag & Drop" 39, 41, 43, 209, 215

E

Electronic Communications Privacy Act 15

I

J

K

L

M

N

O

LaVergne, TN USA
23 July 2010
190625LV00001B/4/P